TESTIMONIALS

"The minute you stop learning, you stop growing. The minute you stop growing, you die. So don't you dare to stagnate. Upgrade to You 3.0 and keep growing, keep learning - and you will live the life you want to live."

Fredrik Haren - The Creativity Explorer

"Being in the cusp of 4th industrial revolution and a major shift in skills in demand, You 3.0 provides a principled approach to not only those looking at re-inventing or pivoting themselves but also a foundation for those just breaking into the modern workforce.

In the past, being a thought-leader may have been sufficient in a niche market, industry or geography; but in a far more globally connected, highly competitive digital world, transcending to influential thought-Leader who's highly visible is paramount."

Callum Bir, Chairman, AI Australia

"You 3.0 is an easy read if you are looking for a quick journey towards your core. I personally liked the anecdotes and stories to illustrate how one can build a successful professional career. Building one's story to building a network and personal branding it covers different aspects of professional growth. Whether one chose to be a thought leader or doer, consistency in branding is extremely important. Great read and highly recommended."

Munjay Singh, Senior Vice President, Infosys

"You 3.0 is not just a must-read but a must practice! We live in a super-competitive world. Not only are we competing with each other we are also competing with ourselves. It is not enough to think about what we know and what must do but we must also think about who we know and how we are perceived. This is hard.

Authors have done a superb job of providing a framework to help individuals systematically plan and navigate their careers.

The book shares wonderful examples and stories which make you reflect on your own individual context. This makes the framework personal and allows you to apply in your own personal context. The book provides practical tips and techniques that are based on well-accepted fundamentals while leveraging the

YOU 3.0

A powerful strategy
to achieve professional goals with
self-discovery and personal branding

ANAND TAMBOLI
AMIT DANGLÉ

SPOTLIGHT
by (N) notionpress.com

No.8, 3rd Cross Street, CIT Colony,
Mylapore, Chennai,
Tamil Nadu 600004

First Published by Notion Press 2020
Copyright © Anand Tamboli, Amit Danglé 2020
All Rights Reserved.

ISBN 978-1-64899-742-6

nuances of social media and modern practices making the book an essential read for every professional."

Anand Deshpande, Founder & Chairman,
Persistent Systems

"You 3.0 will ignite your thinking; it has captured key elements for a new and renewed perspective on life. The world is at a very interesting juncture, and there could not be a better time for us to pause, reflect on who we are, what we are capable of, and could become.

Your brand and your story are extremely powerful assets and are a deep reflection of your essence, with the right toolset, you can grow it exponentially and reap the rewards of the value & wonder it creates. It is these times of rapid change, and you need to step into new discomfort zones. Create a new narrative for your life - rapidly adapt to the emerging paradigm shifts and stay relevant by embracing key lessons from this book. Go upgrade yourself to the latest version of You!"

Anuraj Gambhir, Innovation Catalyst and
Disruptive Techpreneur

CONTENTS

PREFACE

It was the fourth phone call between us that month. The previous hour-long calls, while managing our work and time zones (Anand lives in Australia and Amit is in India), hadn't brought down the interest in the subject. Instead, the feeling of being on the verge of something important persisted.

The broad question that got us thinking was how careers are affected in uncertain times. The world is changing fast. Employers' expectations from employees as well as employees' expectations from employers are changing significantly. Moreover, the classical assumption that merely doing a good job can advance your career is getting beaten to extinction. Along with the right skills, new world order demands you to have a personal brand. Unfortunately, for most of the professionals, this isn't on the top of their list.

There is a saying, *"The fresh crop adapts fast, top rules the nest, and middle adjusts."* Without a doubt, the most affected group in this current atmosphere is the middle management. They are always the first to go through the rigor of unlearning, re-learning, and adjusting to new realities.

So, at the end of the fourth call, we decided to dig deeper.

A couple of frustrating weeks later, our research had hardly yielded anything solid. Typical personal branding advice that we found usually went like this, "Identify your target market, find what they like, consume, or buy. Then polish your offerings and branding to match that."

Our own experience has taught us that personal branding by itself is not absolute. Personal background and long-term aspirations have to be aligned and part of this journey. When you start to explore personal branding without due consideration to these critical elements, it feels like force-fitting. Retrofitting seldom works, and hence there's a weird disconnect.

The result of our deliberation for months was a powerful and practical approach that every professional must understand. With this book in your hand, we feel quite confident that it will help you in setting up that foundation.

There is an interesting pattern in every good comedy. At first, there is a setup, and then there is a punch line. Our professional life is much like that. We keep accumulating degrees, certificates, talents, resources, car, motorbike, house, and so on – all material aspects of life. That's our setup.

Now here is the problem. Most people know what their setup is, but they don't know what their punch line is. Without a punch line, there is no joke. Similarly, without meaningfully using your setup for life's purpose, there is no self-fulfillment and self-actualization.

As a result of that missing aspect, most people remain frustrated throughout their careers without ever understanding why. They live with unfulfilled dreams only because they remain obscure and can't create the necessary distinction. They are unable to identify what their punch line is, so they stay in a comfort zone and keep working on their setup. They keep adding more items to their portfolio. It's an uncomfortable place to live your life in – don't be "most people!"

Our objective is not just to show you a pathway for achieving professional goals, we want you to do it with self-discovery and personal branding. We want to show you how to stay relevant in any disruption and how to focus on the very thing that you can control the best – you, your reputation, and your brand.

We understand that everyone reading this book may not be at the same stage in his/her professional journey. Nonetheless, this book will help you with one of the three ways. If you already know most of these things, it will reinforce what you know. If you have forgotten some of them, it will be a great reminder. More importantly, it will also help you by revealing new ideas and insights for progressing and achieving your personal as well as professional goals.

To make most of this book, you may want to start applying concepts as you read them. Better yet, note down your thoughts, and do the exercises. If you prefer a more structured approach, you can download useful templates from *https://www.anandtamboli.com/youbook.*

It is important to note that the strategy we explain here has a particular syntax. We have sequenced each chapter according to that syntax. For example, building and utilizing your connections and network may not be useful until you've figured out and fine-tuned your story, expertise, and value proposition. Moreover, there is no point in working on visibility if you haven't built a significant network of people around you.

But, none of the content is theoretical. We have applied it in our lives and it has worked for us. And, no matter who you are or what you have done in the past, we believe that everyone has a mountain of value to offer. Of course, you must articulate, package, and showcase it strategically.

What is the point of having a good strategy, but doing nothing with it? Just like any journey, even here you need to take the first step. Most of us feel that we are not cut-out for all this.

Kick out the imposter syndrome, if you have one. Don't give in, just keep going, and it will work. The beginning is always difficult, but if you keep at it, things will improve, you've got this!

Disruption is perhaps the one thing you will repeatedly face during this decade. And every time it happens, there will be a tectonic shift in jobs, the economy as well as work in general.

We encourage you to disrupt yourself and break out of stagnation as soon as possible.

We want you to learn to become indispensable and uniquely useful.

We want you to upgrade yourself and be the best version of you, become You 3.0!

Anand Tamboli, Amit Danglé

ACKNOWLEDGMENTS

For casual Harry Potter observers, Hermione, Ron, and Harry are seen as the main protagonists in the story. But the aficionados know that Voldemort could not have been defeated without the heroics of Neville Longbottom.

The journey so far would not have been possible without our own Nevilles.

We want to start with our manuscript pre-readers, who took the challenge of reading an unpolished, unedited, utterly raw book, and gave us incredibly useful feedback. Two folks, in particular, *Samantha Pickering, and Sudhir Rao*, went above and beyond. They peeked into the world of *You 3.0*, and their feedback resulted in improving the quality of the book by several notches.

You will see that this book does not look like a traditional non-fiction book with blocks and blocks of texts. And perhaps the main reason for that is *Bhagyashri Ghatnekar's* beautiful illustrations that brought life to this book. She was fast to grasp the concepts and deliver imagery in a record turnaround time.

While the individuals were playing their role, corporates were not far behind in supporting us. We would like to call out *Anubhav Dwivedi* and *Sheetal Pote* of *Saviant Consulting*, *Sachin Ghaisas*, and *Maryann Joseph* of *Emtec Inc* in assisting us with the infrastructure and audience. These platforms helped in testing our ideas and getting valuable feedback from potential readers.

Notion Press is more than a publisher to us. We are thankful to have the entire team for standing by us, extending their support, and fulfilling our requirements.

"Gratitude helps you to grow and expand;
gratitude brings joy and laughter into your life
and into the lives of all those around you."

– Eileen Caddy

---

1 | IT'S YOUR TIME NOW

"I was always afraid to talk to you and ask for help! I didn't know how you would respond." This feedback hit the nail on its head and left Anand perplexed. Reading this and several other similar comments left him even more confused and wondering, "Why?"

There was a tradition back those days, especially among college-going students, where you would circulate a slam book and ask others for their feedback or opinions about you. When Anand did that, most of his friends mentioned that they always thought Anand as a difficult to approach and rather too uptight person.

It was puzzling for him, mainly because during his undergraduate studies, Anand was a relatively diligent and hardworking student. Moreover, he would also help others in getting up to speed and tutor them when possible. Anand always thought of himself as a friendly and helpful person. He also believed that others would be thinking of him in the same way. But that was far from the truth. After reading his slam book, for the very first time, he realized – you are not what you think, you are what others think about you!

You are not what you think. You are what others think about you!

Although Anand's opinion about himself wasn't wrong (from his point of view), he did not come across to others like that. There was a stark difference between what others perceived him to be and what he wanted to be. It was all about *perception*.

What others perceive is often based on what they see, hear, and think. Their perception is directly dependent on what they believe. The point is how you present yourself and how people view you – that is the deciding factor for the impression you will eventually leave behind. While you will go about the business of carrying on your life, people will form opinions about your appearance, personality as well as your capabilities.

If you do not like how people perceive you or what others think about you, you must take charge of your perception of reality. Remember that you are in control of your story, always!

It might seem a bit counterintuitive at the outset, as we keep insisting that you must pay attention to what others think of you. In our modern life, people repeatedly tell us don't worry about what others think of you, do as you wish, and like. And we fully agree with that sentiment. However, when you think about business, career, entrepreneurship, and several other things that we focus on in our life, where people around us play an integral role, we think it is quite critical to consider others' opinions about you.

The way this world is changing, economies are transforming, and options to live a good life are evolving, we think you need to start giving some attention to others' perception about you.

Everything is changing! Are you sure?

There is enough information out in the world to cause an overload, especially around the future of work or the future of leadership – literally, the future of anything, and everything. People continuously talk about what is changing and they also talk about what needs to change.

Much of the change is overhyped and keeps people overwhelmed. Fear brews continuously in most people's heads. People tend to think, *"Will I be irrelevant in the next few years? What can I learn or which skills should I develop to stay relevant?"* or *"How can I grow in my career if staying relevant becomes an issue?"*

But most often, we forget the third variable, or should we say constant – what is not changing!

When people have access to resources such as Google and Wikipedia, everyone can become or claim to be an expert – but these are all armchair experts. The problem with these armchair experts is that they don't have the wisdom to know the difference between good and bad information.

Moreover, rapid changes in all aspects are only one-third part of reality. We talk too much about change around us but ignore what needs to change to make those scenarios possible. And, almost certainly, we don't talk about what is not changing at all.

Significant shifts are happening in the global economy and, like it, or not, they affect you, they affect us, they affect everyone, of course. Understanding what is changing will help one in adapting to it appropriately.

But, knowing what needs to change will help you prepare for it. It may also show you several opportunities to exploit if you wish to do so. Having that knowledge can help you proactively work on your strengths and weaknesses. There is one significant advantage. When you understand what needs to change before new changes start making any impact, you get a balanced view of the whole scenario. It not only helps in prioritizing your own goals but also helps in keeping you internally stable and at ease.

In our assessment, some of the things that are not changing are the tribal and social nature of human beings. Moreover, one of the essential things that will not change is what is within you! Your inner core, the crux that makes you – you; that will not change. And, if that is the case, you have an advantage. The advantage of working on something that is entirely in your control and accessible to you at all times. The question then is: *"Shouldn't you upgrade yourself to take advantage of this?"*

You 3.0

Most of us go through a typical career progression, which we have conveniently divided into three phases here. We have numbered these phases in the software version style for making them more attractive.

However, in reality, they are indeed our significant professional versions that are driven by our purpose and means to achieve that purpose. As you will notice, the model has some resemblance to American psychologist late Abraham Maslow's *hierarchy of needs* theory.

	1.0	2.0	3.0
PURPOSE / WHY	Physiological needs	Safety, love, and belonging	Fulfilment, self-esteem, and self-actualization
MEANS / HOW	Education	Employment, work, and trainings	Progression, diversification, and exploration
ACTIVITIES / WHAT	Learning, adapting, and following rules	Groups, socializing, and certifications	Reinventing, rebranding, and experimenting

For a human being, our very first version starts from our birth and lasts until we begin to work and earn for ourselves. During this phase, we have quite a fundamental purpose of our life – to survive and to grow. While our parents take care of our physiological needs, we pursue education as a means to progress further and to upgrade ourselves. While doing that, the focus is mainly on learning and adapting to the world around us; we remain mostly compliant.

The second version comes with an upgrade at the end of our formal education. During this phase, we mostly focus on increasing and widening our safety net, and at the same time, seek love and belongingness. We either pursue employment or start working as an entrepreneur. Either way, socializing, and being part of relevant groups helps us to achieve our purpose. Many of us keep ourselves trained regularly. Achieving certifications and newer skill sets are mostly seen as safety nets for growth in the future professional career.

However, a common issue we have is that the majority of people get stuck in this second version of their career. They never upgrade from version 2.0. It is like they remain locked within some infinite loop. Their groups and friends' circles keep changing. Their socialization takes different twists and turns and they keep churning out several certifications, many times during the year. But that's it! People remain (or choose to stay) stuck in that loop, which is a comfort zone for many.

And, we think that needs to change. There are many reasons why this upgrade is necessary.

First, each individual, who has worked for at least 10 to 15 years or more, has a lot of tacit knowledge that could be highly useful for others. Not only peers and the organization they work for but also in general for their entire industry or practitioner groups.

Second, many people start to feel unfulfilled or incomplete as they begin to cross that 10 to 15-year mark in their profession. It feels that there is more to life and work, but they can't decisively pinpoint what that is. That sometimes builds up internal frustration, and at other times, it merely results in anxiety or restlessness. It is interesting to note that these feelings do not amplify enough to take precedence in life and, therefore, do not motivate them enough to force the upgrade.

Third, most people would remain content with safety, love, and belongingness in their lives. There is nothing wrong with being so; all we want to point out is that there is more to your life. We feel that self-actualization is for everyone and has a vast potential to bring positive changes in your life.

But the fact is, as the world is changing faster than ever, economies are being dressed, and redressed every week, the upgrade would soon become a necessity.

Regardless of that, we think the timing is ripe now for rolling up your sleeves and taking charge of your life for an upgrade!

You need to shift your focus

We understand that for most people reaching and staying in their version 2.0 is quite a struggle. If not a struggle, it is still the safest bet they can take. However, it is not the ideal position to be in and stay there for very long. That is the reason why if you have an opportunity, internal drive, and if you see the benefits of upgrading yourself, then you must shift your focus.

You may ask, *"Shift focus to what?"*

If you refer to the career progression matrix from the earlier page, you will notice that the focus for people staying in version 2.0 is mainly on forming groups, staying in them, socializing, and earning as many certifications as they can. However, the moment you decide to upgrade, your focus needs to change toward reinventing, rebranding, and experimenting.

Reinventing yourself is no simple feat, but if done correctly can be hugely advantageous. Doing so needs enormous focus. And so does the rebranding. We are talking about your personal rebranding – the you. Thus far, your brand has been what others have thought about you by accident or without any (or very little) conscious efforts from you. It must change. You must focus on consciously projecting yourself in a way that you want others to perceive you.

Rebranding is a relatively time-consuming exercise. No matter how good you are and how many resources you have access to, rebranding is a function of time. Staying put for a longer duration and working on your rebranding also needs focus.

Lastly, you need to experiment in the way you will achieve progress and diversification of your skills and knowledge. When you do it, you will be able to attain fulfillment and self-actualization goals. However, random experiments seldom yield fulfilling and quality output. They produce what they are, sheer randomness! If you expect your experimentation to yield something profoundly meaningful and useful, a strong focus will be necessary.

With a strong focus on reinventing, rebranding, and experimenting, you will need to work on your assets, which will help you make that transition. These assets will help you upgrade yourself from 2.0 and also help you to attain better outcomes in your new version 3.0.

Build assets for your brand

In financial planning parlance, the saying goes, "*Income follows assets!*" It implies that more assets can lead to more income, of course, the caveat is if used appropriately! On the contrary, if you fail to utilize your assets appropriately and thoroughly, then that will result in cash-flow issues.

With a similar analogy to your brand, we think there are at least eight critical assets. And, if you use these assets appropriately, you can upgrade yourself quite significantly. This upgrade will be not only sustainable, but also the most satisfying, consistent, and long-lasting. The following list has some order to it, which means, these assets, whenever you begin working on them, would be to your benefit to work them in the same sequence. We will explain our thinking on that a bit later, but first, let us understand these eight critical assets:

1.   ***Expertise*** – Without a doubt, if you are an expert at something, then that would be your significant asset. Almost all of us exploit our expertise to earn our living. It is about your internal strengths – things that make you an expert or better at something. Knowledge gives you conviction and provides validation so that your brand can grow stronger.

2.   ***Your value proposition*** – What do you do for others? What do you offer to the world and who benefits from it become a critical aspect when you start to see it as an asset to nurture? Regardless of your other brand elements and their immaculate nature, what's the point of

having all of that if it remains dormant and is wasted? You must be able to offer something to your followers, community, and industry or profession. What you offer as a person and to whom you provide that is the crucial foundation of your value proposition. If your value proposition is strong, your brand value grows stronger too.

3. **Drive** – Your desire or feeling that gets you out of bed every morning, this is your passion. People believe that the drive is a strong need or want that makes humans act in a particular way. Look at it as your brain chemistry, if you will. Without drive, your brand may come across as dull and partially inauthentic. It doesn't have to be this way. Everyone has interests and passions, and they may be hidden or unknown. However, identifying or discovering them and nurturing them can prove to be positively contagious for your personal brand's power.

4. **Authenticity** – It is your behavioral aspect. Authenticity is about your presence, the way you live in the moment with conviction and confidence, and stay true to yourself. Rough corners and imperfections are part of your personality. You can't hide them by making them appear perfect or like someone else.

With all those good and bad qualities, you are a complete package. It is a must that your audiences embrace you for what you are.

5. ***Your story*** – This is about your history and the back story – Why you see this world the way you see it and how you developed this point of view. When you tell the story and your point of view derived from your experiences, it becomes an undeniable story. You come across as a natural authority that comes from the place you know and have lived in the past.

6. ***Connections*** – For any brand, personal or corporate, networks, relations, and collaborations are critical. These connections can help in amplifying and spreading your offer, i.e., increasing your value proposition faster and better.

7. ***Appearance*** – This asset is more of an external manifestation or we can term it as a wrapper. No matter what your expertise, values, interests, and passions are, if you are unable to showcase them through your appearance, they may be useless. It is about your external strengths – things that make you appear in a certain way. People would often form an impression of you in the first 30 seconds after they meet you, which is why you would want to make the best use of those 30 seconds and create a long-lasting positive impact.

8. **Visibility** – You may have the best skills and expertise, and you may be as authentic as it can get to be. You may also have significant value to offer to others, but none of that will matter if no one sees it. How do you showcase your brand and offer is part of visibility?

These assets, when managed, and nurtured, can work well for you. You will be able to improve on each of them to upgrade yourself significantly.

And work these assets

It is highly unlikely for someone to say that they don't have any of these assets already. For most of us, the matter is to understand the magnitude and quality of these assets rather than their existence itself.

The first three assets, your story, authenticity, and drive, are so fundamental that each of us has them without question. Moreover, if you have been working for at least three to five years, you would have already started building upon your expertise, appearance, and your value proposition. Your connections and visibility would also have been growing steadily.

Regardless of where you stand in your career and how many of these assets you have and at what level, if you are deciding to upgrade yourself, you must start working on these assets. You will have to not only nurture them but also amplify them to be able to work for you significantly.

We have often seen that visibility has played an essential role in your next level upgrade and brand building. However, it has only worked if and only if other foundational assets are in place, and they are of excellent quality. It means whether it is your appearance or value proposition or your personal story, it has to be well crafted and well presented at all times to work for you. You will have to work these assets before they start working for you.

Look at the big picture

If you look at it from a bigger picture perspective, you will realize that it is not just about personal branding for a career. It is more than that. Your life is more significant than your work-life. We believe that when you look at yourself and your assets like never before, you tend to get results that you have never achieved previously!

The new you will undoubtedly help in accelerating your career or moving to better places. However, you will also see more profound changes in your overall life. You will see a noticeable difference in your social standing. You will exhibit quiet confidence that is not too much or too little, just the right kind, and people will notice it. They may not quite get what changed (but some will), but most would like that change and would appreciate it.

We said this before, rebranding, and reinventing yourself is no small feat. When you make this upgrade work for you, it will boost your confidence like never before. You would have found a formula to make positive changes in your life, all by yourself.

You will realize that this upgrade is not just an upgrade in itself. It is much like a snowball effect. Once you do it, it keeps happening and accelerating in a loop-like manner. So, anything you do after that will be a lot easier than before. You will be able to figure out complex relationships that affect and drive your brand reputation, inside, and outside the work environment.

Most people see personal branding as a goal or an end in itself. Perhaps that's the reason why many people loathe it. The same happens with many things in our life. If we start looking at means as if they are an end in themselves, disappointment is all we would get.

However, when we shift the perspective and see the bigger picture, it looks natural and obvious. Do not look at the brand building as a one-point exercise or destination. It is something you would use as a means to an end. You will be achieving something through this exercise. It will be your life upgrade, which will be satisfying as well as mostly irreversible.

If what we have said so far is resonating with you, then we think it is time to stop your reputation from having a life of its own and take control of it.

It's your time now – take the first step and do it!

KEY TAKEAWAYS

- You are not what you think, you are what others think about you!

- How you present yourself as well as how people view you – both are important.

- Remember that you are always in control of your story.

- Understanding what is changing helps you to adapt while knowing what needs to change helps you to prepare for it.

- Your critical assets are *expertise, your value proposition, drive, authenticity, your story, connections, appearance and visibility*. Work on these assets before they start working for you.

2

EXPERTISE – SOURCE OF CONVICTION

SKILLS

"An expert is a man who has made all the mistakes which can be made in a narrow field."

– Niels Bohr

And, we agree with Niels Bohr. If you have made enough mistakes (if not all) in a specific field, you are indeed an expert. Wikipedia defines expertise as elite, peak, or exceptionally high levels of performance of a particular task or within a given domain. An expert is someone with broad and in-depth competence in terms of knowledge, skills, and experience through practice and education in a particular field.

Your expertise is not only essential but also critical for your brand, as much as all other factors that we are covering. It gives you conviction and provides a type of social validation so that your brand can grow stronger.

Your source of conviction

Much of your branding and upgrade have a higher dependency on your expertise, and without being convinced yourself, it is almost impossible to convince others. So, where do you get this conviction?

You can undoubtedly derive it from your purpose of being, that is the cause that *you stand for*. But that will only get you so far, and if you think long-term, you need more than just the purpose. Expertise is one such thing that will help you do that. With knowledge and purpose, you don't have to convince others much, instead imbibe it in your persona for others to believe in you.

Master of all

You may have heard this often as people often revile those with multiple fields of expertise by saying, "*Jack of all, master of none!*" That was mostly true in the past decade or century maybe, not anymore. With the proliferation of technologies, tools, and access to knowledge, you can be a master of several things. In fact, due to the convergence of technology and many other fields, it has become a necessity to be master of all while staying "*Jack*" of all too.

However, there is a catch. Don't overdo it by falling into the trap of knowing something just enough. We often access information on a particular topic and go deep to understand it more. Once we have gone deep enough, it often feels that we are almost an expert in that topic and people feel an urge to call themselves an expert about it. It is a dangerous trap and often backfires and we strongly advise against it. And there is an easy way to curb it.

Whenever you work on any particular topic, check for the depth of your knowledge. Additionally, evaluate if you have had practical experience in that domain long enough to have seen the entire business or domain cycle and understand it completely. If not, then stay away from calling yourself an expert in that domain. You may have gained some knowledge and information about it, but that is far from being an expert. Developing meaningful insights takes time and significant depth and breadth of experience.

However, it is perfectly alright to have expertise in multiple domains by sheer working experience and functions of time. If that is the case, go for it. Again, hold back yourself from claiming expertise in more than three domains, at least in the beginning. Doing that will enable you to focus on the important ones that can add value to your profile as well as to your audience.

But be aware! The problem is with someone having multiple areas of expertise, not with the person itself. It is the audience that has difficulty recognizing talent and being able to relate with you quickly. The best way to approach this issue is to prune the list of expertise and find common ground among the ones you shortlist. Then use the umbrella term to identify your expertise instead of using the narrow niche.

Doing this will help people in seeing some congruence and stop them from getting confused with what you do and your expertise.

What is thought leadership?

There is no specific definition of thought leadership. We think one of the ways to explain thought leadership is that it is a type of content marketing, which uses your talent, passion, and expertise to cater to your community, and provides the best and most profound answers to the biggest questions that your community is asking. It has to be done in the format of preference of the community or audience.

At its core, thought leadership involves stepping out of the comfort zone and taking a futuristic view of an issue that you care about the most. Doing this requires not only interrogation but also demands a strong constitution. It also needs the ability to marshal the right people and align them around your perspectives, which is often challenging. However, if you succeed in doing that or even start making such an impact, you will see your brand soar rapidly.

If you are an expert in something, your chances of becoming a thought leader in that domain are much higher. With a new decade of disruption upon us, micro-niches are becoming accessible and relevant.

Thought leadership advantage

For several decades, people have visualized a career in a pyramid-like structure. You start at the bottom and rise to the top, only a few get to become leaders and the rest of us follow the herd.

With emerging technologies and the fourth industrial revolution, this pyramid structure is getting disrupted.

It will not look like a pyramid anymore. It is getting flatter and tribal. If you have been following agile or similar working models, you will already know that.

People start working at an entry-level and soon become knowledgeable workers. The next advancement happens when you become a functional expert. While most of us get stuck at this stage, a few manage to become subject matter experts. And, this is where people stay for very long or sometimes forever. However, if you have chosen to upgrade yourself and move to the next level, you are looking at becoming a thought leader.

We often measure our lives with different parameters of success; for example, work-life balance, money earned or saved, happiness, and level of self-fulfillment.

With the entry-level job, our focus is on getting the experience and building up the resume, so we accept a little bit of grunt work. As our knowledge and expertise increases, only the income goes up. With functional expertise, we start to feel better, money is okay, but we still struggle with work-life balance. Becoming a subject matter expert only gives some more money, nothing else. Expertise is essential, but going above and beyond can be highly helpful.

There is another interesting aspect, which defines these levels. The bottom two levels are solely dependent on *what you know* – your knowledge level decides where you fit. The next two levels are dependent on *who you know*. Your network, relationships, and contacts start to play an important role here. However, if you must move beyond that, *who knows you* may become the most critical aspect.

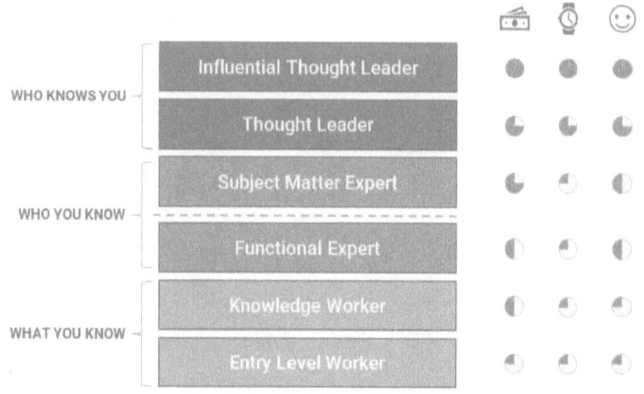

Crossing the line between functional expertise and becoming a subject matter expert is relatively hard. If you do that, you are already better placed to move toward influential thought leadership, but only if you commit to becoming one and are ready to work toward it.

Take a moment and locate your current position in this hierarchy and decide where you want to be. If there is a gap in your aspiration and current situation, we think it is time to change your approach.

You will notice that expertise is a pre-requisite for becoming a thought leader. But not all experts can become thought leaders. Only those who build their intellectual property portfolio and original ideas can get to that stage – thought leaders are creators of original taxonomy and content.

Thought leadership gives brand affinity, whether it is a personal brand or commercial one, the results are the same. When you demonstrate thought leadership with your expertise, you become part of the larger conversation and your audience will like that. It is one of the best ways to allow your audience to get to know you better.

How you can be the one

We have seen many people who carry the self-proclaimed title of thought leader, especially on their social media profiles. Sometimes, it is a mere result of their close circle calling them so or at other times they are aspiring thought leaders. We often strongly advise against doing that – adding that title in your profile.

First, you must validate those people who have bestowed that title on you.

Are they way more qualified than you to do that? Are they respected thought leaders from your industry? Is that a title bestowed upon you as an award?

Second, under some unique circumstances, doing that might be okay, but unless that is the case, we recommend not doing that. After all, thought leadership is less about the title itself and more about how other aspects of your professional success pan out.

Three significant aspects are at play in becoming a thought leader – positioning, publications, and collaborations.

Get your positioning right

It is the first important step in maximizing your ability to influence. It is vital how you articulate your value proposition to others. Being able to communicate what you stand for, your values consistently, and your contribution to the world has a profound impact on your positioning. Your positioning eventually determines why people should listen to you and what do you have that they need.

Ask yourself – What are my values? What do I stand for? What can I offer that isn't obvious? What can people learn from me? Everything you do and say must align with these questions. Authenticity is one of the critical characteristics here.

When your positioning becomes more explicit, it will show up consistently in your online and offline persona. It will help to further strengthen your positioning and build up an active profile.

Start publishing about your area of expertise

Regularly publishing your ideas, relevant and useful content in your domain of expertise, and original ideas can add to your credibility.

However, where your ideas and content are published also plays a vital role in addition to who publishes them. Creating relevant, useful, thorough, elegant, and unique content can help in attracting potential collaborations and amplifying your message.

Depending upon the quality of your content, the level of perceived authority you have in your industry can increase. As a thought leader, your thoughts, ideas, and intellectual property (IP) become your products. Publications will help in leveraging your value proposition commercially. More inbound opportunities will come your way as you start establishing your authority, along with increasing your credibility.

Don't forget to collaborate

While excellent positioning and portfolio of publications can help you become a well-known subject matter expert, it would be highly limited. You must amplify your value proposition so that it reaches the maximum number of people to make a meaningful difference in your industry and everybody's life.

By collaborating, you come across as an honest broker for making a positive difference. Moreover, just like any other brand, you will need amplification to increase your impact. Connections are essential in this aspect.

Influential thought leaders are not the ones who know something, they are known for knowing something.

Stay away from quasi thought leadership

If you look around, you will see that many people think or call themselves as thought leaders, but they are not necessarily true thought leaders. Many people get two out of three principles right or just right. There are three kinds of quasi thought leaders.

The first kind is people who get the positioning right and they do have several good collaborations. However, if they haven't proven anything by publishing their thoughts, ideas, IP, or they don't have good valuable and useful content out there, then it is a sheer waste of their positioning as well as collaborator's time.

The second kind is people who regularly publish much content in terms of blogs, videos, podcasts, and many different mediums. They also have access to various collaborations to maximize their content. But then again, if they don't stand for something substantial with their positioning, then that's a problem. More often, you will notice that their positioning keeps moving in line with the trends in the market. They are simply trading their content to monetize from it and may not add any value to their community, industry, or society.

The third kind is people who have got their positioning right and they often publish excellent valuable content too. But they don't actively collaborate with others to spread their message and thought leadership. They remain subject matter experts or unknown geeks. A good valuable insight, idea, or IP gets limited outreach and never makes a high positive impact.

Becoming a thought leader is a significant undertaking, so be prepared to make that effort and stay away from pseudo expertise.

Thought leadership and personal branding

To put in perspective, thought leadership is a strategic step through which you showcase your expertise. On the contrary, an own brand is what will hold it (your thought leadership) in its place. They are both complementary. Nonetheless, going from thought leadership toward personal branding can be more manageable. Given that you already have substance, polishing it becomes easier.

While personal branding is all about *who knows you*, thought leadership is all about *what you are known for*.

Just like a three-legged stool, personal brand and thought leadership stand on three crucial aspects: positioning, publications, and collaborations.

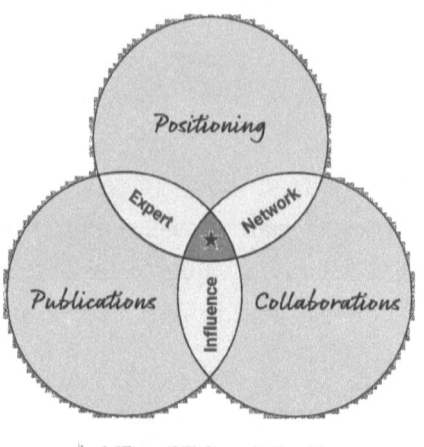

⭐ Influential Thought Leader

In late 2019, we surveyed hundreds of professionals, wherein we invited them to answer a few questions on these three aspects. The average scores based on their answers floated around 3 to 3.5 on a scale of 1 (lowest) to 5 (highest). Specifically, positioning scores are 3.5 average, publications scores are about 3.2 average, and collaboration scores stand at 3.6 average.

It means, on average, people we surveyed seem to be stuck in the middle! They work in the zone of being functional and subject matter experts. It is quite a tricky position because if the majority of professionals are in that zone, it is the most crowded place. Differentiating within that crowd is extremely tough.

Combining personal branding with thought leadership can give you that leverage to stand out from the crowd and take charge of your life, upgrade yourself quickly, and successfully.

Difference between product and personal branding

The question wasn't unexpected, but Amit still had to think through to answer it accurately. "Humans are not objects or products. They think, feel, and have emotions. So there must be differences between the branding of a product and a person," commented a lady during one of his presentations. Her slight irritation was understandable as Amit was exemplifying personal branding with product branding examples, which he thought was a more natural way.

The critical difference is a product is created and branded to the taste of the audience. The process of product creation involves market research, design, and engineering to give it specific features and offer particular benefits. Personal branding is about connecting with the audience with an 'existing' product. A product can have infinite iterations based on market feedback. With each iteration, the benefits of the product and brand positioning can change. Humans can't adapt precisely to the expectations of the audience. Much of the success in personal branding depends upon a seamless story involving your strengths and weaknesses, aspirations, and experience, as well as skills and flaws.

However, managing and executing activities that make the audience feel the way they do about your brand are similar in product and personal branding.

Expertise is not a point in time

Expertise is not a point in time achievement. You don't become an expert at something and then do nothing afterward. It is an ongoing endeavor. You not only need to improve and hone your expertise, but you also need to expand your zone of expertise. It is not only a logical progression but also a sustainable one.

So, how can you do that? Well, the most profound, and obvious step you can take is to keep reading relevant literature. Online or offline, the format doesn't matter. The idea is to keep yourself informed of the current state of work in your domain of expertise.

Expertise is not a point in time achievement – it is an ongoing endeavor!

As you nurture reading, you can't just stop at that. When you read, there are three things you can do with that information. You can ask yourself, *"How can I use this information and utilize it to inform my audience?"* You can also ask, *"What do I think about this information? Where do I agree and where I don't? And why is that?"*

We think the second question is more helpful for your own sake. The first question doesn't elicit any original response. It is rather rhetoric; you will only share and curate information or content created by others. On the other hand, when you add your perspective to that information and customize it for your audience, then that becomes your original creation. As long as you use proper attribution and references, the content is yours. It is your intellectual property now. And as you keep doing this regularly, your IP portfolio on a particular subject matter keeps growing. It builds your expertise and makes you more valuable to your audience, day by day.

It is also worthwhile to back reading with writing. Doing it will not only help in the dissemination of your views but will also assist in fine-tuning your thinking. Every time you write, you think, and rethink – this feedback loop helps in shaping your perspective and honing your expertise. Writing should follow seeking feedback from readers and the audience, understanding their views about your contribution and stand. Work on relevant feedback and keep improving.

Over time, some of the aspects of your expertise may become redundant, i.e., go out of business, or trend. For example, if you are an expert in a particular programming language, within a year, that language may become obsolete or less popular. However, logical thinking, higher-level abstractions, and algorithms, in general, won't be archaic as such, at least not so quickly. Build your expertise around these aspects so that you can sustain them longer.

Be uniquely useful

Upgrading your personality and professional (or personal) life takes a lot of conviction. Expertise is one of the sources that can help you build this conviction.

People have asked us in the past, *"What if I don't have anything unique to offer?"* Our answer to that is straightforward – it is not about being unique for the sake of being so. You don't always have to be unique, but you can still be uniquely useful. It can be your expertise, but you will have to identify it, work on it, build it, polish it and, most importantly, present it to the world.

You can't always be unique, but you can still be uniquely useful!

KEY TAKEAWAYS

- Your competence gives you conviction and provides a type of social validation to help your brand grow more potent.

- Career progression goes through three key stages, defined by three key aspects – what you know, who you know and who knows you.

- Thought-leadership gives brand affinity and it is complementary to personal branding.

- When you demonstrate thought-leadership with your expertise, you become part of the larger conversation.

- Expertise is not a point in time achievement, it is an ongoing endeavor.

- Every time you write, you think and rethink – this feedback loop helps in shaping up your perspective and honing your expertise.

- You can't always be unique, but you can still be uniquely useful!

3 | YOUR UNIQUE VALUE PROPOSITION

"I don't think it's good that we're perceived as different, I think it's important that we're perceived as much better."

– Steve Jobs

"So, what do you do, mate!" Matthew asked Anand during their introductory meeting at a meet-up. Anand could have said anything from what he was working on that day to what he generally does in his business. Perhaps he could have told Matthew about his designation and role description in the company. But, none of that would've mattered.

Why is that? How can this seemingly simple question be so hard to answer? The reason is the implied inquisition behind this question. Matthew's actual question seeks what Anand's offering to others is; he wants to know Anand's unique value proposition.

Regardless of your other brand elements and their immaculate nature, what's the point of having all of that if it is for nothing? You must be able to offer *something* to your followers, community, industry, or profession. This *something* is your value proposition that is unique to you.

What you offer as a person and to whom you provide are the crucial foundations of your value proposition. If your value proposition is strong, your brand value will also grow strong.

Value proposition for an individual – why?

For quite some time, value proposition was a buzzword that was applicable only in the corporate environment. Not anymore! Crystallizing and developing your value proposition further helps in many different ways.

First, it helps in establishing yourself as an expert in your field. It establishes not only your expertise but also your authority and the value you offer. This further strengthens your reputation and perceived value in the marketplace.

Having a strong value proposition can help set you apart from all the others you normally compete with. And, if you can harness the power of social media effectively, it can also help increase your credibility. This success spiral can boost your career as well as wealth and health significantly.

Given that your value proposition can greatly help in building your reputation and brand, it is imperative that you focus on creating one.

Being different and valuable

People often distinguish the psychological aspect of a brand from its experiential aspect. While the psychological aspect is dependent on symbolic construct within the minds of others, the experiential aspect comprises of all interactions with you as a brand.

If you think further about your value proposition as an individual, it would be easier to plot it across two dimensions of desirability and differentiation. If your value proposition is unique and desirable, you will almost be indispensable. Your overall value proposition will be very strong.

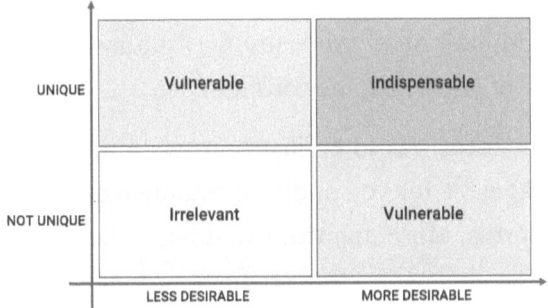

On the contrary, if your offering is weak or commonplace (almost like a commodity) and it doesn't have any differentiation, you might find yourself in the zone of irrelevance sooner or later.

You must offer something that is uniquely valuable and desirable; that's the key to being indispensable. However, we want to make it clear that this differentiation has to be beyond mere novelty. It must offer real value. It should also be difficult for someone else to replicate it, which will help you maintain your differentiation for longer periods of time.

For the people who lack one of the two aspects, their skills are easy to replicate; therefore, this makes them highly vulnerable to any market force changes. However, people who lack both aspects are in a grim situation. They often find themselves prone to becoming irrelevant – don't be a resident there!

Being indispensable, however, doesn't mean you have to burn yourself out entirely. It only suggests that you have to apply the above model judiciously. Select your unique value proposition carefully and in the context of your customer or audience.

Your focus has to be just narrow enough so that it is manageable for you and broad enough to have scope for progress. More importantly, it has to be adaptive in nature so that when market forces change, you don't find yourself in a quagmire, stuck, and immovable.

Making your offering adaptable

It means you will have to adapt your value propositions continuously. Typically, every three to five years, you will find that significant adjustments are necessary as trends would have changed.

Nonetheless, every time you adapt, and change your offering, it must resonate and align with your strengths and principles. The best option would be to keep receiving feedback from your audience or your customers. If you nurture this habit (of continuous feedback), adjustments would be very easy and they would be seamless.

Getting it right

Perhaps the most grueling question everyone would face is what should be or what is my value proposition? We often feel that whatever we repeatedly do as a part of our work or our skillset is our offering. It is not entirely true, and we think it is a rather very narrow way to look at this in such a manner.

More importantly, how to develop your value proposition so that it is more desirable and unique is crucial. In general, we think there is an appropriate sequence that you can follow.

Relevant – No matter what the first and foremost criterion is, what you offer to the world has to be highly relevant and useful. Without relevance, it won't resonate with your audience or customers. Consider it to be a foundational trait of your value proposition, it has to be relevant to be valuable.

Thorough – Once you find a relevant offering that resonates with your customers or audience, then you can develop it further. Make it as thorough as possible, go deeper. The more thorough you make it, the more valuable and desirable it will be.

Elegant – Only when you make your value proposition relevant and thorough, it would make sense to work on it further. Making it elegant will make your offering extremely valuable. Doing so means you are now on the verge of becoming indispensable.

Unique – While your offering grows, develops further, and strengthens, it will become more valuable. You will have immersed yourself in doing this in such a deep manner that you will start finding intricacies and develop new perspectives. It will help you in bringing your unique perspectives to the offer. And, that's when you will develop an exceptionally valuable and unique value proposition. Most likely, this is when you will find yourself in the top right quadrant. You will be indispensable.

With these four steps, your value proposition not only gets better, but it will also soar to a new high.

Your traits are important too

Besides the core offering as a skill set, perspective, or advice, we have noticed that how that offering is delivered is equally important. It is dependent on personal traits.

Ask yourself, *"What is unique about the way I provide this value?"* This perhaps could be your characteristic way of delivering your work. Your work and your trait, together, make your offering even more unique and are crucial for making you desirable.

Think about your unique strengths, talents, and expertise. Ironically, we find it easier to identify those strengths through the negative lens.

Here is an example. People often called Anand *judgmental*. Being judgmental is seen as a negative trait. However, the exact opposite of judgmental is accepting everything as is, which clearly Anand isn't. And when you look at that trait with an analytical mindset, Anand cannot accept each, and everything as is, that simply is not his nature.

Now a careful consideration of this trait (of being judgmental) will reveal that when not done in moderation or in wrong places, it has a negative impact. However, using this in moderation and judiciously can become a strength. When Anand used it properly, people started to call the same trait as *discerning*, which is still the same, but a better version of it.

Similarly, if you think, or people say that you are too emotional for a given role or profession, don't try to toughen up. That's not you! Instead, see if that can be replaced with being empathetic. When you transform such traits, they become catalysts to your value proposition and make you more desirable and authentic. This way, you won't have to change yourself; you just have to represent yourself better.

Packaging your ideas

We find this as one of the overlooked aspects of value proposition. Quite often, people have a lot of ideas, unique perspectives on a certain subject matter that could become their unique value proposition. However, simply because they fail to package it properly, it goes waste.

There are several ways in which you can present or offer your perspectives and ideas to others. You can write about them, speak about them, or show, train, and mentor others on them. These are the most common ways to showcase your value proposition to your audience or customers. Pick any of these that suit you or are comfortable with at the beginning and package your offering accordingly.

For example, if you have unique perspectives or experiences on change management challenges and methods, write about them so that more people will learn about it. You may choose to speak about them in public so people get to hear your views and see what you have to offer. By doing so, you will be able to showcase and advertise your value proposition.

This type of packaging is quite important because without this, your ideas, views, and concepts will remain in your head forever. They will be limited in their reach and won't help you in establishing your reputation whatsoever.

Once you package your offering, it becomes easier to monetize it. Otherwise, what's the point of having a unique value proposition if you cannot use it for your economic or professional benefits?

Having more than one value proposition

First, let us clarify that it is absolutely normal to have multiple value propositions for an individual. We are often told to go an *inch wide and mile deep*. That is having highly focused expertise and go deeper. Which, in general, is true when developing your value proposition, but not quite applicable once your offering has been crystallized.

The world has seen enough number of polymaths (multifaceted personalities) that are revered. Be it Leonardo Da Vinci or Thomas Edison, they were all polymaths and had multiple offerings to the world.

However, developing and handling multiple value propositions is not a small feat. It is a high-risk endeavor that, if you handle well, can yield multifold benefits. If you feel quietly confident about handling many of them simultaneously, go for it. Don't listen to others who would not help you do it anyway. But, be very careful as minor problems in one lane can result in major problems in all the others.

Having more than one value proposition is acceptable if you handle them carefully and smartly. Even better, if you can logically connect them all together, it will make your life easier as well as help others to see them congruently.

We have seen that despite being many, congruent ideas are easily acceptable and are often seen as more valuable.

Discover it, package it, deliver it!

You must take your unique value proposition needs through three phases, all being equally important.

First, you must identify or discover your offering. And, when you do that, you must codify it so that it gets crystallized and easier for you to deliver reliably and repeatedly. It will also need just enough fine-tuning for impeccable delivery.

Second, your offering needs to be packaged very well for you to be able to use it professionally and personally for your benefits. Without packaging, you won't be able to share or deliver it.

And third, you must deliver your offering to your target market, audience, or customers. Stay in a close loop with your audience, get their feedback, and hone your value proposition further. The ultimate success of your offering is in successful delivery and until that happens – you must keep going!

KEY TAKEAWAYS

- You must be able to offer *something* to your followers, community, industry or profession. This *something* is the value proposition that is unique to you.

- Your unique value proposition helps in establishing yourself as an expert in your field and strengthens your reputation.

- If your value proposition is unique and desirable, you will almost be indispensable.

- Your focus has to be narrow enough to be manageable and broad enough to have scope for progressing.

- Don't change for the sake of it, represent yourself better.

- To establish your reputation, package your ideas, views and concepts appropriately.

- Having multiple value propositions is acceptable, if you can handle them carefully.

4 DRIVE – YOUR INTERNAL ENERGY

"We don't have any stock of this component, sorry!" The store manager told Anand in one breath. During his stint at LG Electronics, Anand was working on a high-value project that had strict timelines.

It was one of the dream projects he was eyeing for several years and there was absolutely no way Anand was ready to let go of that on account of the shortage of one tiny component. His project was scheduled for pilot trial in two days and not meeting that timeline would have impacted severely on the entire schedule. It was a matter of successfully demonstrating his management skills for critical projects like this. Since it was one of his dream projects, Anand was very passionate about it and had this incalculable drive to make things happen.

So, Anand and his colleague decided to take a different approach. They knew that the required component could be purchased from the retail market at a higher price to get the job done. They hired a cab and headed to Mumbai, 200 km away from the LG factory, to get the required component. That day they traveled approximately 400+ km to get the component and deliver it to their assembler. It was almost midnight by the time Anand and his colleague achieved what they wanted to accomplish that day.

It was perhaps one of the longest days for Anand as he continuously hustled through the day. And, there was only one thing that kept him going – his passion for his dream project!

These things don't happen often, but when they do, only one thing keeps you pushing forward – your internal energy and your passion!

Without passion or drive, you, and your brand may come across as dull and partially inauthentic. It doesn't have to be this way. Everyone has interests and passions and they may be hidden or unknown. However, identifying or discovering them and nurturing them can prove to be positively contagious for your brand power.

Drive – an intrinsic force

We can see *drive* as a natural force or energy that challenges you, intrigues you, and, most importantly, motivates you. Drive does all of this together. It is the force that pushes you away from a little leisure and pleasures to do something more meaningful and value-added in your life. Mind you, it is not about doing what you love, but something that makes you do things that you choose to do.

What drives you will wake you up in the morning and get you out of bed. If a particular cause or objective drives you, it will help you navigate and fight the toughest challenges that you might face.

However, most importantly, the drive will make you more exciting and livelier on the outside. Although it is an intrinsic force, its effects manifest on your face, in your behavior, and eventually in outcomes that result from your actions. It is the combination of desire and energy directed at achieving your goals.

Why is it important?

Taking a step to update your brand and overall approach toward life is not a small feat. It requires high levels of motivation to do that. Motivation is nothing but the desire to achieve a goal in life.

Motivation can be external or internal. However, you should always prefer internal motivation. Your passion, the internal drive is the starting point for your motivation. It will help you focus on specific goals and pursue them effectively. External factors can further enhance your drive.

It plays a vital role in personal branding as it helps in setting meaningful goals and objectives. Not only does setting goals becomes easier, but also achieving them, and staying ahead during tough times comes from this drive. At times, a personal upgrade journey may seem more frustrating than otherwise. Your drive and passion will help in achieving the same.

Let's see why drive matters to a professional with an example.

Companies are cautious when they hire sales and marketing personnel. A wrong selection can impact revenue numbers severely. In his initial days as a sales and marketing leader, Amit's selection criteria considered years of experience at the top. He soon realized that in fast-paced markets such as technology, just higher experience isn't enough. The team must have the drive to learn new technologies and adapt to new demands.

To validate his assumption, Amit kept track of the career progression of some of his team members. He observed that among people holding similar years of experience, those with higher drive had twice the chances of being promoted than others.

Your brand and your passion

When upgrading yourself, your drive can provide the necessary fuel for it to work effectively.

So, the first thing you should be doing is looking at your habits. Do you get enough sleep, eat well, and exercise regularly? How about smiling and laughing every day? All these things have an impact on your energy levels and, therefore, on the personal drive. Taking care of yourself is not an option; it is a fundamental requirement for you to perform at your optimum level, do your best, and stay enthusiastic about the work you do.

Then, get a check on working habits. Are you a workaholic? Do you run in autopilot mode all day without doing anything new or exciting? Do you find yourself doing just enough to keep your head above the water? Do you drag yourself to work every day? If that is the case, you may be stuck in a rut; you must change your approach and do something about it.

Begin by taking the initiative, look for something new, and challenging. Reflect and take a hard look at your career and goals of life. Doing this might need you to change the way you look at things, your outlook, and your perception about life and career as such. Change in perspective is highly necessary as it will have a direct bearing on outcomes.

Passion – superficial or profound?

People often ask us one question, *"How do I know which of my passions are temporary and which are real?"*

The question is reasonable as having mixed passions is entirely plausible.

Here is a quick test to figure that out. When you think of doing something that you are passionate about, just the thought of doing it will make you smile. If that is the case, it is most likely that it is your real passion. Any superficial passion won't yield that kind of emotional response.

However, if this test isn't working for you, check how much you have invested in your passions, monetary value as well as time and energy. Subconsciously, we often avoid spending too much on something short-lived or that we are not entirely convinced about it.

Nurturing passions

Just having a passion or drive is not enough; you have to nurture it and grow it. Make it your strength and use it against your weakness. There are several ways to nurture your passions.

Get more involved in your passion: Doing this means you can build on what you have and spend some more time to go deeper. If you are passionate about cooking, maybe you would want to take cookery classes or learn from the Internet. Then try making things at home and feed others, seek feedback, and improve. You don't have to stress on it, have fun – this is your passion, not another work project.

You can join other communities that inspire you and support your passion: Engage with others with the same interests and mingle with them, whether it is do it yourself (DIY) stuff or photography or boating or something else. Do your thing and then go do it with others.

When necessary, take a pause: If you find yourself in a loop, it is better to pause rather than keeping moving. Take a step back and reflect. Your passions are supposed to make you feel passionate (duh!), not miserable. Take a break and circle back when you feel like doing so.

Passions can change over a period

Passions can evolve as your life progresses and you go through different stages of life. Each stage shows you something that you didn't know before and can leave you with a new passion. However, that doesn't mean you will lose enthusiasm for the previous passion. It instead gets added to the list and the things you are passionate about grow.

So, the answer is yes, and no, your passions would change over a period – but not by turning off one and getting the new one. They will get added to your passion list.

It, however, may affect your brand if you don't handle it properly. People who follow you and know you for your passion may question you and could get confused. Confusion often can lead to dropping off from your followership. Therefore, each time you pick up a new passion, make sure you can link it with your overall bigger purpose and have a strong reasoning story behind it. It will help people understand your new passion by seeing it in the right context and therefore strengthen your brand instead of weakening it.

Spread your message faster

Now the critical question you might ask is, *"How can I use my drive, my interests, and passion to spread my message faster?"*

At times, we see that people's passions are not directly related or connected to the work they do. That's completely okay as they don't necessarily have to be like that, although passion about the job often makes it easy. If that is the case, if your passion is related to the job, you can use your story to share with your audience and show them what inspires and drives you. They will be able to understand you better and will also see more congruence in your overall persona.

However, if your passion is not directly related to the work you do, that is not a show-stopper. It just means you need to make some effort to connect the dots by showing others how your passion and work bond. Naturally, different people will perceive your story differently. And, they don't have to agree with your passion or interests at all times too. But disclosure can be quite helpful. If not directly, they might help you indirectly in pursuing your passion. Perhaps they know someone who shares the same passion as you and they can introduce you to that person. This help won't be possible if you never share what drives you and what your passions are. Of course, do this in moderation.

As you share your passion with others, they can see what extra you are bringing to the table. In addition to the unique skills and expertise that you are offering them, you will add a cherry on top with your passion, which can make the difference. You will notice that as you disclose your passions and what drives you, it will help you make an active emotional connection with others and spread your message faster.

People will not only relate with you better, but they will also help you in pursuing your passion by assisting you in any way they can, of course, the essential requirement is you must share your passion with them.

Talking about your passion

If you wish to showcase any of your traits, one of the most preferred ways would be telling a story. Think about a story that demonstrates your passion. The better you sound while narrating it, the more impact it will make on the audience or your customer.

However, typically, as passion is an internal driver, it is easy to get caught in your interest and ramble a bit about it. To avoid this rambling, break your approach into a few steps.

Begin by telling briefly about your passion. When you meet someone for the first time or have a short time to explain, briefly stating your passion can help. In one of the tools we teach for elevator pitch design, this forms a quick and high energy introduction. You can say, "*I love {passion}. I love it because {tell more about why you love it – the top first reason is enough}. Due to this, I can {explain what you achieve due to your passion}.*"

For example, Anand would say, "*I love helping people become self-sufficient and stay in control of their lives and career. I believe that one of the critical components of happiness is having a sense of control over our life. Due to this, I can make people feel grounded, calm, and in full control, which makes them happier."*

Try writing yours based on this template. You don't have to follow it to the *'t'* afterward, but to begin with, use the template as it is and then improvise.

The good part is you can easily merge this statement in your social media profile summary. Talk to your friends, family members, and ask them what they think. Based on their response, you may fine-tune it further.

It is not an elevator pitch, but a part of it. You may have passions that are personal and business or work-related. Use them appropriately depending upon the circumstances and audience.

At this stage, the next person may get interested in listening to you more and that's when you tell them more about how, with your passion, you help others. They may probe you further asking, "Wow, interesting! How do you do that?" That is when you add more details about your passion and describe how you do what you do in some more detail. However, be careful not to start rambling, keep it short, and straightforward. Tell them enough to understand what it is, but tell them just enough to pique their interest.

If your passion is resonating with them, they will ask you for more and that's when you get your conversation going. Tell them more about your passion – why you have it, how it all started, and how you nurtured it. Remember, you are having a conversation here. Go about it accordingly. It is up to you to get into more details or keep it short.

Besides, telling others about your passion using a story, you can also demonstrate it in different ways. For example, if you are passionate about any particular sport, likely, you are already playing it. Maybe you can showcase your achievements in that sport to others, who need to know more about your passion. Perhaps, you can speak or write more about those experiences and mix them (moderately) with work.

Passion is internal energy!

Yes, indeed! Your passion, your drive, is the internal energy that keeps you going.

Among several other things that we learned throughout our upgrade journeys is – personal upgrade needs direction, but more importantly, it needs a potent driver to propel oneself in that direction. Without an internal drive or passion, it becomes a long drag and people drop off before the finish line.

To avoid that from happening, find your passion, articulate it, and nurture it. Use it to connect the three big dots – what you do, why you do, and how you do it!

KEY TAKEAWAYS

- Without passion or drive, you and your brand may come across as dull and partially inauthentic.

- Your drive is a natural force or energy that challenges, intrigues and motivates you.

- If you change the way you look at things, your outlook, and your perception about life and career as such, it will have a direct bearing on the outcome.

- Your passions may change over a period, but they usually get added to your passion list.

- To strengthen your brand, each time you pick up a new passion, link it with your bigger purpose and have a strong story behind it.

- Disclosing your passions will help you make an active emotional connection with others and spread your message faster.

- Use your passion to connect the three big dots: what you do, why you do and how you do it!

5 AUTHENTICITY – A SIMPLIFIED PERSONALITY

"Authenticity, for me, is doing what you promise, not being who you are."

– Seth Godin

One of the biggest misconceptions floating around about personal branding is a belief that it means to "create" a public image of yourself. Nothing could be further from the truth. It is not about adding a new persona; instead, it is based on what is real, genuine, and unique about you, i.e., authentic! You cannot be someone who you are not.

With authenticity, you will be working on uncovering your true self, not fabricating something else. People often feel that for being an appealing brand or personality, you must have a fine-tuned and sharp, magnetic persona, which, according to us, is not the mandate. The rough corners and imperfections are part of your personality. You cannot hide from them by appearing perfect or like someone else. With all those good and bad qualities, you are a complete package. It is a must that your audience should embrace you for who you are and what (perfections and imperfections) you come with. Any pretense will always fail in the future, which will quickly destroy your brand.

Recently Elon Musk took a shot at Bill Gates on Twitter, tweeting that his conversations with Gates had been "underwhelming." Musk's remarks came after Gates gave an interview saying he had bought a rival electric car.

Both are billionaire American business magnates on the course of changing the world. Post Microsoft, Gates has become a philanthropist and wants to find cheap cures to deadly diseases, while Musk wants to elongate human survival with Tesla, Solar City, and SpaceX.

The similarities end fast when it comes to their personalities. Gates is more erudite, while Musk is brash. Gates is subtle, while Musk carries the air of supremacy.

The above incident reflects their authentic nature. Musk didn't waste a breath to criticize Gates. And Gates never rebutted Musk's tweet.

Unfortunately, any deliberate attempt to build authenticity or to come across as an authentic person often backfires, do you know why?

You cannot be someone who you are not!

Authenticity in this context

While the somewhat technical definition of authenticity is around transparency, vulnerability, and integrity, we believe that authenticity is way bigger than that. It is not a quality you have, but the one you demonstrate every single time you interact with the world, directly or indirectly.

And, therefore, it also means showing deep conviction and confidence at any given moment.

Staying true to yourself is crucial. If you are authentic, people around you will feel that vibe and will be at ease. Have you ever visited someone's home uninvited? How did you feel when they saw you and let you in? If that person was your best friend, how did you feel? And, if that was not a best friend, just an acquaintance, or new friend, how did you feel? Did you feel awkward in the latter case, and not so much in the former one? If you have felt at ease and comfortable with your best friend, that's the closest example of how an authentic persona can make people feel.

There is another perspective to authenticity and it compares one's actions with one's beliefs, desires, and personal value system in general. If your actions are congruent with what you believe in, you will most likely come across as an authentic person.

In general, transparency, vulnerability, and integrity are common foundations for being authentic. Your behavioral congruence with your beliefs, thought process, and values decide your authenticity.

When delivering your personal story, the level of conviction you demonstrate and values it exhibits can tell a lot about the authenticity of your brand and persona in general.

Why is it important?

Every person is part content and part personality. Content is perhaps easier to generate and still has a competition to face with Google, Quora, LinkedIn, and alike. But the personality is unique to you.

Sharing your story is an act of inclusion. Embrace your story; don't hide, be authentic. There was a time when credibility was wearing a suit with a tie. Not anymore. Today, you can demonstrate credibility by being authentic. People will believe and trust you if they can relate to you. They will believe you more if they can see an unedited version of you – scrappy, raw, and vulnerable personality comes off as real, relatable, and genuine. It might go contrary to the conventional belief and a lot of advice that is out there – offline and online.

In our personal experiences, whenever we presented ourselves as "polished" and over-rehearsed in our presentations, people thought something wasn't right. Most of the audience was unable to pinpoint what exactly put them off, but those who commented stated that they thought the appearance was a bit inauthentic. Whatever they meant, we believe as a normal human being, we are bound to have minor imprecision and rough edges that would show up now and then. And, if people miss that part, their BS (Bullshit; basically the mental ability to realize when a person is lying) detector switches on. It may very well be a false alarm, but they can't tell the difference.

That doesn't mean you need to be deliberate in making mistakes or adding some imperfections.

You won't have to do anything for that, just being yourself would suffice.

Moreover, a super-polished and perfectionist persona often puts an invisible barrier between you and others. Emulating perfection backfires. If people can't connect with you, they won't be able to relate to you, they won't feel you as trustworthy and eventually won't buy from you or hire you.

A double-edged sword

A word of caution here. Always remember that authenticity is like a double-edged sword. If you decide to concoct a persona for the sake of your brand and if it doesn't have any foundation in your life's reality, you are aiming for your foot. You will be shooting your own foot if you follow the *"fake it until you make it"* advice. These types of efforts usually have the reverse effect that will not only confuse but will also disappoint others.

Don't believe in the "fake it until you make it" advice. This is not acting. Get real!

How authentic are you today?

Let's do a quick self-check. Being authentic is something everyone wants to do, but not everyone succeeds.

Do you stay true to yourself at all times? Did you ever try to be like someone else? If you have been trying to imitate someone else, you may miss being authentic.

Are you self-aware and are mindful of your thoughts? Do you know why you think and what you think? Do you know what has been the premise of your thought process and beliefs? Authentic people often say yes to these questions.

Do you overtly try to *fit in*? If yes, you may have been losing on being authentic. We understand and acknowledge that we must adapt to our surroundings for survival, whether it is corporate environment, social surroundings, or a real environment. Nonetheless, our reference to *fitting-in* relates to those corporate and social settings where you can survive without *fitting-in*. If that is the case, you don't need to overdo it.

Ask yourself, *"What do you truly believe and what do you think you believe only because you heard it several times?"* Now, shed all those beliefs that you've found on inputs from others. If you have too many opinions derived from external information and other people's thought processes, then you are not authentic.

"To be authentic, we must cultivate the courage to be imperfect – and vulnerable. We have to believe that we are fundamentally worthy of love and acceptance, just as we are. I've learned that there

*is no better way to invite more grace, gratitude,
and joy into our lives than by mindfully practicing
authenticity."*

– Brené Brown

How do I build an authentic persona?

One of the critical components of an authentic persona
is derived from congruency in your behavior.

Congruency of your behavior depends on how
present you are and how you are responding to the
person you are talking to. If you are not present in
the moment, your facial expressions and responses
get delayed by a split second. The next person can
unconsciously detect that difference or delay and then
they tag your behavior as incongruent. It, in turn, leads
them to believe that you are inauthentic.

Being attentive is the best way to display your
authenticity. By being present in a moment while talking
to someone, you show them that they are essential and
you respect them talking to you. This courtesy goes a
long way.

Your persona mostly consists of five different
aspects:

1. ***Invisible image:*** As the name suggests,
    others can't see, and neither can you. It is your
    internal system – your values, beliefs, and
    thought process. It is unique to you.

2. ***Assumed image:*** This is what people will think about you or expect from you before they see you for the first time.

3. ***Visual perception:*** It is your visual presentation; do you look as you portray your personality invisibly through your thoughts and beliefs? Do you dress appropriately and look the part?

4. ***Experienced image:*** In your presence, while interacting with you, what kind of experience do others get?

5. ***Proven image:*** Once people have known you for a long time, how do they average out your personality? Do they see you as someone who walks the talk? Do they identify you for something or with something?

These are just a few high-level aspects that project your persona and authenticity is the foundation for that.

To begin with, start making your decision consciously and give some forethought. Make sure that you are happy with your choices and you are ready to take full responsibility for those.

Decide your goals, short-term, or long-term, based on your purpose of life. Don't make those decisions based on societal or peer pressure. That would be a good start.

Stand for something

One of the best ways to build and exhibit your authentic self is to have a point of view or core value. Stand for that and cultivate it. The question you might ask here is this – What should I stand for or what core value are we referring to?

To put it differently, it is about the uniqueness of your personality. Deep down, everyone cherishes specific values and they would also feel more passionate about something more than other things in their social and business lives. When that is the case, these personality traits, cherished values, and characteristics you are passionate about represent your brand.

Your brand is the reflection of the type of person you are and want to be in the future. It is also a reflection of your core values and motivators. Eventually, these things drive your behavior on a day-to-day basis. The way you represent yourself on social media, online in general, and offline has a direct dependency on these values and motivators.

Personal brand, especially authenticity, can be quite tricky to explain or exhibit, let alone to amplify further. How do you handle it in a way to make it simpler to explain? How can you make it easier for others to understand and relate? The answer is – by standing for something!

We recommend you take a few steps to achieve this. Start with your core values – values that you would want to be associated with and can show them through your behavior. For example, do you appreciate honesty as a personal value? How about integrity? Do you value both equally, or one has precedence over the other? If you can decide on 3 to 5 values that you would want to associate with and cherish, that should give you a short and usable list of authenticity that you stand for.

Once you have figured out the top few values, it becomes way more comfortable to focus on them and find out several ways to keep them on top of your mind. Additionally, you can take conscious efforts to show these values in your behavior on a day-to-day basis.

Additionally, we also suggest that you give enough time for reflecting upon these traits regularly. It will help you keep a tab on how you are performing. Ask yourself, *"How am I living the values that I cherish so much?"* See what you need to do to make them visible through your behavior. So, for example, if you cherish honesty as a trait, live that trait, say it aloud, and assert it in front of others, whenever there is an opportunity. Over a period of time, people will associate you and your brand with that trait. They will be convinced that you stand for honesty. That's the goal!

It is also a good idea to pick up a few role models to follow – not in a literal sense but for particular traits.

For instance, one of Anand's role model is Thomas Edison, the inventor of the light bulb. Among many other characteristics, people also know Edison for his tenacity and persistence. And when people know that Anand sees Edison as his role model, they subconsciously associate Edison's traits with Anand. So, when Anand says that he stands for tenacity and persistence, it is easier for people to believe him.

Keep in mind that you should pick up more than one role model to follow, perhaps three to five is good enough. The reason for that is, not one person will showcase all the values that you cherish and stand for. Additionally, the idea here is to refer to some of their traits, not to copy them ditto.

Sometimes when you stand up for something, you may have to go above and beyond regular routines and take some risks. Maybe you will choose different careers or domains to work based on your reflections or you will perhaps want to leave the job and start working as an entrepreneur. It is possible that you may refuse to do something at your workplace or in social life if it doesn't align with your values. Whatever it may be, it will surely attract some attention from others and if you stay true to your values and assert them positively, people will respect you for that. However, when you decide to take such risks, make sure you are clear about consequences and have a plan to handle them. Also, make sure that you accept these risks pragmatically so that you get rewarded and not miss out on opportunities.

When you use your brand and your values as life's GPS (global positioning system), then it will not only inspire you but also others around you.

Authenticity comes from three factors

As we highlighted this before, authenticity comes from three factors – *transparency, vulnerability, and integrity*.

Being transparent about who you are and how did you get this far makes you relatable. Personal disclosure is helpful. Being vulnerable is a risk and letting people know about your struggles, hardship, and difficulties that you encountered along the way is equally important. When people see your vulnerability, they respond to it, respect it, and since it forms a kind of mental investment, they feel more personal and relatable. They become more responsive.

If you use them strategically and consistently throughout your messaging, it will work better. However, as in any general advice, more is not always better.

If you start to get into too many and too much detail, it might have an opposite effect and can put people off. Vulnerability doesn't mean you are required to expose your dirty laundry. Transparency or vulnerability – do it in moderation, just as much as necessary to do the job.

Integrity, on the other hand, is more of a foundational concept. You can't imagine an authentic personality without having integrity. Without integrity, authenticity is questionable, and often fake. Earlier, we mentioned congruence in your behavior, thinking, and values. It is of utmost importance to maintain that integrity. You must do what you say you will – walk the talk.

Don't push it too hard

Common sense must prevail and be moderate in whatever you do by applying *phronesis* (an ancient Greek word meaning wisdom or intelligence) at all times.

There are times when it is not the right time to be vulnerable. For example, imagine a situation where you are leading a team and everyone is hard-pressed with the delivery schedule. Your team just missed one. Under such pressing circumstances, everyone needs your leadership; they would want you to stand up for them and help solve the problem. Of course, everyone will be under pressure, including you. However, this is not the time to be vulnerable and disclose it to everyone that you are equally worried and feeling the pressure. You would instead acknowledge the situation and show everyone that although you are concerned, you are confident. You will have to show that you are in control, lest everyone goes berserk by knowing that their captain too is lost.

Authenticity, though a simple concept for an individual, has a high dependence on receivers. That means you will have to experiment to figure out the balance before you maintain those levels of transparency and vulnerability. Integrity, on the other hand, has to be undoubtedly 100 percent at all times.

Sustain and nurture

It is perhaps slightly easier to figure out one's true self and make peace with it. However, sustaining that persona and nurturing it further takes strength. We are (unfortunately) required to wear a social mask and adopt a persona to identify ourselves with. But, right beneath that persona sits our true self, our authentic self. And, if you have found that out already, you must happily remove the persona that you have been carrying around and retain your authentic one.

Don't identify yourself with the fake persona that you have been carrying around for a long time. Being authentic is not about wearing a better mask for that matter. It is about shedding the mask completely! Wear the inherent goodness and stay true to your innocence. Once you find it, sustain it, and nurture it.

Keep simplifying

In 2017, Adam Grant, an American psychologist, and the author was interviewing Facebook COO Sheryl

Sandberg at Wharton, when he asked her a question related to personal branding[1]. She argued that personal branding is an overblown craze and people shouldn't do it. According to her, *"People are not that simple. We are not packaged. And when we are packaged, we are ineffective and inauthentic."*

We partly agree with this sentiment. We recognize that personal branding is an overblown craze, but that's not the reason not to do it. We all agree that people are not that simple; in fact, we are one of the most complex and complicated animals on the planet. And that's where we think personal branding plays a vital role in turning that complex animal into a simple human being.

Remember, your brand resides, and exists in the minds of other people. There is no physical existence. And it is an important concept to understand that your brand is a concept. As your brand exists in the imagination only, everything you do (or don't) affects it. It gets affected by what others think about you, believe about you, and feel about you. In essence, your brand is whatever comes to people's minds when they think of you.

And, if that is the case, don't make it too hard on others. Keep it simple and congruent with your

---

1. https://www.youtube.com/watch?v=Qym57Nx Pwg4&t=1850

true nature. Then continue and keep simplifying it. Remember, simple things are easy to remember and easy to recall.

Authenticity is a simplified personality.

KEY TAKEAWAYS

- Don't try to be someone you're not. Keeping actions congruent with beliefs helps in building an authentic persona.

- Transparency, vulnerability and integrity are three foundations for being authentic.

- Every person is part content and part personality. Content is easier but has a competition to face. But your character will be unique to you.

- If people can't connect with you, they won't be able to relate to you.

- Your brand is the reflection of the type of person you are and want to be in the future.

- Maintaining integrity is of utmost importance. Do what you say you will – walk the talk.

- Being authentic is not about wearing a better mask, it is about shedding the mask!

- Your brand is whatever comes to people's minds when they think of you. Don't make it too hard on others.

- Keep your brand simple and congruent with your true nature. *Authenticity is a simplified personality*.

6 | WHAT'S YOUR STORY?

"Life stories do not simply reflect personality. They are personality, or more accurately, they are important parts of the personality, along with other parts, like dispositional traits, goals, and values."

– Dan McAdams[2]

When we are talking about your story, we are mostly interested in your personality. Your story, its aftermath, and your experiences are unique to you. They are one of the significant assets while building your brand and giving your persona a solid foundation. Your back story characterizes you. It is loaded with heaps of information about how you have become who you are. All our experiences help us grow; they cause changes. Therefore, it is quite essential to recognize and hone your back story.

Your back story characterizes you and is loaded with heaps of information about how you have become who you are.

Why do you need one?

You will agree that most people work well with others whom they can relate to quickly. They will go above

---

2. McAdams, D. P., & Manczak, E. (2015). Personality and the life story. In M. Mikulincer, P. R. Shaver, M. L. Cooper, & R. J. Larsen (Eds.), APA handbooks in psychology®. APA handbook of personality and social psychology, Vol. 4. Personality processes and individual differences (p. 425–446). American Psychological Association. https://doi.org/10.1037/14343-019

and beyond if they can identify themselves with you. People say that trust comes from personal disclosure. So, how do you share that kind of information with others? It can't be in the form of a traditional bio-data or resume. There has to be a bigger story, the one that defines your present.

When upgrading yourself and building a personal brand, your story will be the first point of click, and people naturally want to know – who you (really) are? How can you help them? They also want to know how do you know what you know, i.e., your journey to this point? And why should they trust you? And, do they share anything in common? When you know this about yourself, you will realize that finding a better career option will become easier. You will become more effective in communicating your value no matter what you do.

The above questions are the linchpin for making meaningful connections with other people as well as doing business. If you can do this well, people will eagerly engage and will be more open to doing business with you.

And, more importantly, the art of storytelling can be traced back to the beginning history of human life. In today's world, where information overload is standard along with memories such as goldfish and shorter attention spans, we need to be more tactful to get our message across and stand out from the noise. Which story do you think can be more authentic than the one of your own?

If you are having trouble being heard, understood, or recognized for what you are and what you do, then there may be an issue related to your story.

In turn, it also means people have an issue with your identity – generally speaking, they don't get you! It is not your fault; it is just a communication gap that is causing a significant roadblock.

Many of you would acknowledge the importance of being searchable and discoverable in this hyper-connected world. When you are on the phone with someone for the first time, you both are likely searching for each other online. If you are going for a meeting, people will seek you online. If you met someone recently, chances are that they will search for you online and so would you. The point is, if you take control of what comes out in search results, you can better write your future.

Now, we are not saying that your story is equivalent to your online profile. However, what we are saying is that if you don't tell your story explicitly, people will make their own version of your story. And, we are sure that you won't like their version of your story.

Your story – what is it?

So, what is a personal story (or stories) anyway?

Your stories are a set of your life-changing experiences that shaped you, emotionally, experientially, exponentially, and at the core. Given that narratives are one of the best ways to put some orderliness to unordered experiences, we recommend using the story or narrative format to weave those experiences. When you do that, they form your story, or set of several stories.

In general, say for someone of 30 years of age, that person must have had millions of experiences throughout those 30 years of life. However, not all of them count or impact who that person is, what that person believes, and why that person thinks so. If you feel you have had an average life so far, there would still be at least 50 such incidents that you remember would have made some profound impact on you.

When you start organizing past experiences into a narrative or story form, you will notice something interesting. Such that even if you thought that you were living your life as randomly as possible, enough things would have happened so that patterns would start to emerge[3]. And therefore, when you look and think hard enough for incidents that changed your life and thinking fundamentally, you would be able to find one.

If we ask you to narrate an incident from your past life that changed your thinking permanently, how would you look for one? Here are three questions you might ask yourself to get to that point.

What happened? – Describe the incident in a few 100 words. In short, tell us the critical details of that real story.

What did it mean to you? – Whatever happened, several perspectives are possible. But from your point of view, what did it mean to you? It typically should come out as one or two-line learning from that incident. It is critical learning from that incident.

---

3. Infinite monkey theorem, https://en.wikipedia.org/wiki/Infinite_monkey_theorem

What was that all about? – The crux of the matter. If you were to put one or two words around all that happened, what would those be?

Let us take an example from Anand's story that we started in the previous chapter. In that story, we briefly described what happened.

Learning from that story for him was clear – *"You are not what you think you are. You are what others think about you!"* That's what it meant to Anand.

And finally, he believes that it was all about "perception."

There you go. Now you see why we say what we say and where we come from about this perspective. We are sure that this was just one of many other stories that shaped up Anand's point of view about perception. Nonetheless, it clearly shows how incidents in our life can leave an everlasting impact on our inner core.

As such, you should have several stories that give you clarity about your viewpoints. Additionally, there would also be many stories that would highlight your qualities, the ones you want others to know that you have, but don't know how to demonstrate beforehand. Telling them your story when using those qualities can be a powerful way to achieve that revelation. Therefore, you must start writing down and cataloging these personal stories for your future use.

Now the question is, "How?"

How to find key personal stories?

One way you can easily find several personal stories is by asking three critical questions, as described before. Apply that to any memorable incident in your life and you will have something to share. Especially stories that make you believe in something and why is that so.

Besides that, we also recommend a few trigger questions that could incite your thinking:

1. *What is the biggest challenge that you have faced so far and how did you overcome that?*

This story is about your redemption, where you faced a challenge and you overcame it. You are the hero of that little story. Think about what made you successful in doing that and highlight those traits. Such stories can be educational as well as motivational.

2. *What is the best lesson that you have learned from your class teacher, mentor, or any other influential person?*

We reckon if the lesson is coming from your class teacher, it will be a highly impactful one. This is because you still remember it after several decades. Just imagine how many life's decisions will have been affected by this impact or lesson and how many will in the future? It mostly will be gold, and you should share it with others.

3. *Do you have any favorite superheroes? Why are they your favorite?*

It might seem like a simple question for a moment, but it isn't. Although we are talking about a fictional character, the reason why we resonate with one aspect and not with several others can tell a lot about our preferences about others. Maybe you like physically superior personas, or perhaps you prefer brainy people more, or maybe it is about being able to do something that is never done before. Whatever that is, find it and describe it. You will be amazed to see how you reflect that same choice in your real life.

4. *If you have done several jobs or gigs in your professional life, which one is the best? Why?*

Let's face it, not all the jobs we do are perfect ones and we don't like them all equally. We do some of those only to get by and the others are a dream come true. Regardless, why you loved any particular job or gig can tell a lot about your preferences and what you value most in your life. Sometimes, we take things for granted and we do not understand what exactly we want from a job or project. But in hindsight, we can figure out patterns and what made us smile. This story can be a good narrative for telling others what you truly value the most.

5. *When growing up, what did you want to do in your life? How does that square with what you are doing now?*

You can spin this story either way. If you are doing what you always wanted to do, then this is your success story. If this is not the case, your reasoning behind the difference will give some insights for the next generation. It will also tell others how you are making peace with reality. It should showcase your maturity and realistic way of looking at life.

6. *Talk about the funniest incident from your past, the one that changed the way you think and feel about something.*

Sometimes these stories form useful icebreakers in networking or an introduction set up. At other times, they can illustrate simple lessons in funny and memorable ways, and can still have deep meaning.

7. *Did you change careers in the past? Does your formal education differ from what your current profession is? How did that happen?*

These stories can talk a lot about your adaptability. They tell how you deal with real-life challenges by being flexible and continuously learning.

8. *Did anything ever happen to you out of sheer luck? How did you respond to that and what did you learn from it?*

There are some instances in our life where the unexpected happens. The story maybe you get lucky or unlucky. Either way, it tells a lot about your character and how you handle entitlements.

9. *Is there any profound moment that defined your professional success?*

If you take a careful look at your trajectory of life or career, chances are you might have changed significantly in many years. How did that happen? At times, it feels like a natural evolution, until you think deeply and find out that it isn't really. Did you make a significant shift from your earlier path and why did that happen? There might be a lesson or two that others might be interested to learn from you. Think about the process you went through, your conclusions, and outcomes.

There are no hard and fast prescriptions here; several different ways and combinations are possible. Regardless, in all these situations, you should focus on three core aspects and questions – What happened? What did it mean to you? What was it all about?

The reason to focus on three questions is simple. They give you an extract of the prolonged version of your story and package it in a shareable form. This will be handy when you use your stories to communicate your brand.

How to write about failures?

"I have not failed. I've just found 10,000 ways that won't work."

– Thomas A. Edison

Most of us can count more failures than successes in our life. We all make mistakes, we fail, but some people use mistakes to build great achievements. Failure allows you to come across a new idea that you otherwise wouldn't have encountered or it makes you a better person.

If you have such inspiring stories, make sure to articulate them. These tips will help you portray your failure story as a growth opportunity and occasion for achievement:

1. Select an event where you experienced failure, inadequacy, disappointment, or defeat. Describe how you blew it up, but use your "failure" to demonstrate the rise to success and character building.

   Example: Amit was leading a team to build a computer tablet for the rural market. The tablet had many innovative features, including the ability to charge using built-in solar panels.

The product failed in the market because of the higher than expected price.

2. Explain how something went wrong. Share insights on how the failure happened and what steps you took.

   Example: The final product price escalated due to development overruns and misjudged procurement cost. Also, the product appeared when preferences were changing from tablets to mobile phones. Amit and the team had a fantastic piece of technology nobody wanted to buy. Luckily they heard of a project initiated by the Reserve Bank of India called Financial Inclusion, where thousands of rural people were allowed to open zero-balance bank accounts. The tablet was a perfect device to collect customer information from the field.

3. What did you learn from the experience? How did this change affect you personally?

   Example: Even with the changed positioning and use, the tablet eventually didn't fetch expected revenue for the company. Amit learned the divine truth – it's just not good enough to be innovative. The pace of innovation should be in congruence with the market demand and customer spending power.

How to tell your story?

Having stories from your past that you can tell is a great start. Now you need to use them in your communication with others appropriately to see their impact. Here are a few things that you should consider when telling your stories.

Being able to narrate your stories powerfully, whether verbally or in writing, can help you build trust and shared understanding with your listeners. This ability is a great asset to have.

When you are telling stories that have other characters, accentuate them. Don't forget that despite being your story, it is not all about you. It is about how you fit in the overall big picture. How you collaborate work and get along with others? How you interact with other characters in your story and how you treat them? What did they get while being part of your story?

You have to show your fundamental values and characteristics that you want others to acknowledge and appreciate. Whether it is your strategic thinking, decision making, wit, wisdom, or your ability to think in a crisis and setbacks, remember you could have told the listener about all these characteristics just by stating them, saying that, "I am a strategic thinker." But that is not any fun, and that is why we are persuading you to use the storytelling method. It is not just telling your audience or customers that you can do something, but demonstrating to them your real and authentic story.

Do not fill the communication with just a sequence of facts, speak about the rationale behind the actions that you took or other characters took. Shake up some emotions. More importantly, share your point of view. Share how you see things and why you see them like that. Highlight your unique perspective and where you derived that perspective from.

When you have a relevant story, use it to explain why you see the world the way you see it. What happened, what did it mean to you, and what was it all about? Speak with authority; after all, it is your own story that you experienced in your life.

At times it will be necessary and useful to show evidence that your story is for real. How to do that can depend on several factors. If there is something that you can show or prove with numbers, news, or metrics, it is fantastic. But if there isn't any, it will be better to think through and be a little innovative and find ways to add realistic elements. Nothing can be more frustrating when you tell a real story from your past and people see it as a made-up one.

Every time you tell your story, you will discover something new. Most of the time, it will be about how people respond or react to your story and what common questions they have? What intrigues them and makes them interested in you? These are the things you can use to your benefit when connecting with others.

Every story has a time and place to tell

Just because one has several personal stories to share, it doesn't mean one can throw away stories any time at any place. We understand that you would be careful not to do that. But there is something more – appropriateness, relevance, and substance to telling a personal story.

Every story must fit snugly to any given situation at all times. If that doesn't happen, stories can become boring soon. If you're a good narrator, you may end up entertaining the listener, but then it would only be that. There won't be any impact. Sharing stories is about having a purpose. Why are you sharing your particular story? What does your story prove? And how does it relate to your current situation?

If your story has a triumphant end or has an element of redemption of some sort, then it would make sense to use that story to establish your credibility. These stories can be easily summed up as success stories and are powerful to boost your credibility.

On the contrary, if you are trying to build a rapport, relationship, or trust, then you might prefer to use stories that have tension elements in them. An obvious caveat here is that you should have done an excellent job in those tense cases to release or ease the tension. Alternatively, the story that has an element of tragedy might help too. Again, hopefully, you would have done an excellent job of overcoming or flipping the tragedy.

Remember, some things happen to people and cannot be redeemed ever. If that is the case in some of your situations, we would strongly recommend avoiding such stories. Having redemption themes in the story of your life generally indicates greater well-being. If there is no redemption in your stories, then the opposite might be true. You wouldn't want your listeners to be de-motivated or lose interest in you.

Our entire purpose of honing the story of our life is to connect at a deeply personal level and establish a common ground. Always use an appropriate story from the set of your life stories.

A caution against so-called personal branding experts

In the past few years, the personal branding industry has thrived and, unfortunately, started muddying the waters already. We have seen so many people being turned off by humble-bragging that is a continuous disguising act of self-promotion.

Some self-proclaimed gurus would tell you to indulge in acts of self-promotion. They ask you to create (not identify) your unique value proposition and construct a persona around it. The act of creating a persona around the value proposition is what puts us off in the first place. It is much like putting the cart before the horse.

Your persona is not a point in time of your life. It is your life – your past, present, and most likely, your future too. How can you expect that to be carved out for a specific unique value proposition?

Your persona is not a point in time of your life. It is your life – past, present, and most likely, your future too.

Instead of doing that, why not understand where you come from and what has formed your thought process, how it shaped up you as a person, and what you care about in life as a whole? Once you put together your (real) story, then you can highlight your critical traits through it and serve the listeners. Remember, when someone asks, "What's your story?" They are not doing it to please your ego, they want to know more about you and find common ground to connect.

If you pay close attention to this fundamental aspect of storytelling, people can identify with it as their own. When you do that, no more push tactics or efforts will be necessary. People buy from people they can relate to or connect. Once you do that job honestly by adhering to the process, results would follow.

If you are interested and have time to listen to all the so-called personal branding experts, you can do that. But, before you take any step, undertake a rigorous validation of what has been said and asked to do. Whatever you do with your reputation, it is mostly a one-way road, so be cautious!

What about those untold stories?

Several stories of our life remain untold. We get that sometimes there are valid reasons for keeping them that way. But every untold story has some power to hold your feelings hostage. Imagine how you would feel if those are released and you can make peace with them. Keep those stories as *FYI* (for your information). Use those untold stories to reflect on your life and appreciate the transformation you see, how far you have come, and the backbone that you have developed along the way.

You don't have to tell and share those stories that you're not comfortable with. Nonetheless, do not ignore them. Identify such stories and acknowledge them. Think and learn from them and then keep them aside. Doing so will give you two things – first, the quiet confidence that you have learned your lesson and you won't let mistakes repeat, and second the ability to defend them or rationally clarify them if ever they come to public attention.

How will you know if your stories are working well for you?

Well, you will know simply by telling them. We know it is not that straightforward, but it is almost that simple.

The good part about your story is that it is flexible. You are both the main character and the narrator. So, if you are in doubt, narrate your story to your friends and ask for their feedback. Ask them, when you tell a particular story, what do they think of you? Then see if that is what you intended to convey. If yes, you're good, but if not, dig deeper and ask them what made them feel that way and see how you can fine-tune that aspect from communications or language perspective so that you convey precisely what you want to.

So, go ahead, tell your story

Remember, you are infusing facts with feelings to make a good story that is real and yet connectable. Get a grip on your struggles, setbacks, hardships, triumphs, tensions, tragedies, and revelations. Narrate your stories with confidence and humility. Tell your listeners why you are telling what you are saying and show them why you are the way you are, what you have to offer, and how you are already the most eligible one with a real example? Now you know 'why,' you have the tools and you have the ability. It is time to work on them and tell your story!

KEY TAKEAWAYS

- Every significant experience will help you grow and change you profoundly.

- Your back story characterizes you and has heaps of information about how you became who you are.

- If you don't tell your story explicitly, people will assume their version.

- Always focus on three core aspects and questions for your story – What happened? What did it mean to you? And what was that all about?

- When you share your story, share how you see things and why you see them like that. Highlight your unique perspective and how you derived that perspective.

- Whenever you're sharing your story, understand why you are doing it, what that particular story proves and how it relates to your current situation?

- Your persona is not a point-in-time in your life. It is your life – your past, present and, most likely, your future too.

7 | BUILDING AND UTILIZING CONNECTIONS

There can't be a leader without followers.

"I don't know why I'm receiving all this hate. I'm not even remotely an anti-vaxxer," said Jay sincerely. "I'm worried all this talk will badly hurt my practice," he continued.

Amit knew that Jay wasn't exaggerating. The best asset of a medical practitioner is the reputation, and Jay's reputation as a pediatrician looked almost at stake with all the accusations Jay has been receiving on social media.

Jay had a burgeoning practice as a pediatrician. He was caring and sympathetic to the kids who visited his clinic. Over the years, he started noticing the trend that new generation parents are increasingly paranoid when the sickness lasted more than a few days. The human body is not like a machine that can be repaired instantly. Let it heal on its own with little medical intervention, Jay would explain to them.

Some parents agreed, but still, there was a large group who blatantly asked him to prescribe antibiotics for faster recovery.

So, one day, Jay started posting his views on popular social media sites. His posts centered around how frequent use of antibiotics can weaken a child's immunity system. Jay's first few posts had a handful of views, but they increased fast. The responses were critical of the posts, even some accusing him as a child killer. Jay ignored them for a while. His every new post would bring a new barrage of critics at the doorstep. He has been mistakenly labeled by the Internet as the anti-vaxxer doctor. Not knowing what to do next, Jay had called Amit to help him with the situation.

The first thing Amit noticed that no one had taken Jay's side even after having hundreds of parents who agreed with him. "Do they even know you are making these posts," Amit asked. Jay nodded negatively.

That was perhaps the biggest mistake Jay had committed. The Internet is judgmental, period. A few negative responses can turn the tide of masses against you. The only thing that stands between you and detractors is the wall of supporters. Jay shouldn't have jumped directly to social media. His first task was to take his close network into confidence.

Jay changed his strategy and created a messaging group of parents. He started explaining to them his point of view on antibiotics. He took their feedback on how messaging can be sharpened without being misinterpreted. Involving the close network gave him the confidence to go back to social media to rebrand himself as a doctor against the overuse of antibiotics.

That's the power of connections!

Your brand may need you to share knowledge or you may want to be among others with similar interests.

Having a large number of followers, subscribers, or friends on social media is one of the crucial factors in personal branding efforts. Using tips in this chapter, you should be able to build and utilize more followers.

Generally speaking, a connection is a relationship between people of similar interests. In a transaction with a connection, you act either as a receiver or a giver. As a receiver, you can gain knowledge or access to resources from the giver and vise-versa. By this logic, you will realize that not everyone you know is a connection as such. It is especially true if you consider the transaction being of professional nature.

Loyal followers are a subset of your connections and they will always be interested in engaging with your posts, sharing your content, recommending your ideology, and eventually helping you elevate your social or personal standing. They will stick with you in the face of competition. Their passion gets rubbed on to others to turn into loyal followers.

Additionally, the total number connections are also meaningful as they give a bird's-eye view of your popularity to an outsider. The ideal scenario is to balance both because the success in one feeds on to the other.

So, let's talk about how to build a good network, online, and offline. You may already know how to do most of these. We will talk about leveraging existing connections in greater detail later. But first, let's briefly touch upon how to get started.

The first step is to identify where you can find them. These could be meetings organized by a local chapter or online group on social media. Once you know where your potential connections linger, start showing up there. Let people have a small whiff of your existence while you analyze their activities. Keep a short and exciting introduction ready when people start approaching you. Show your interest in the topic by asking relevant questions. The understanding of participants and frequency of meetings (or posts) will determine if you should invest your time there or head for another pasture.

Out of the hundreds of places where you may find them, choose only a handful if you want to give justice. You may find it tempting to go to large gatherings or groups, however making yourself seen there will be immensely difficult. We suggest that you go for small or medium-sized meetings or groups where people are knowledgeable and approachable.

While you are building connections at a steady pace, don't forget the reason for their existence. You eventually want to project your brand to your contacts and their network.

As an authority in a specialized field whose expertise is sought by others, your first task will be to prove to the world that you are the one. In the pre-Internet era, it meant publishing a book or writing in a newspaper to establish your credibility. Imagine going through the lengthy process of convincing editors or publishers, then months of copyediting and proofreading activities, and finally hoping that readers flock to your book. Today, you can bypass most of these steps with your website or blog. Although the primary challenge is to get enough people to visit and like it.

Interestingly, to attract an audience to a website or blog, the journey begins from the offline mode. People who have depended only on the Internet to reach out to an audience have failed to garner enough support. Thought leaders use more than social media to build their brand. They go through the rigor of a step-wise approach involving personal connections to start with. Now that you have seen how to approach and make connections, let's see how you can leverage them with a technique called *Ripple Effect*.

The Ripple Effect

Let's understand the process of using the *Ripple Effect* to build your followership. If you drop an object in a liquid, it creates ripples. As these ripples spread, the outer waves take a bigger wavelength until vanishing completely.

Imagine that your network is like concentric waves surrounding you. The object dropped is your messaging, which gets carried from one wave to another. Stronger messages will produce more significant and long-lasting waves. You may want to create the most significant first wave, but there's no way to bypass the laws of branding (or the laws of Physics).

It is clear that waves start small, and each wave acts as a multiplier. Let's look at how you can use this effect to reach the right audience.

Starting the ripple

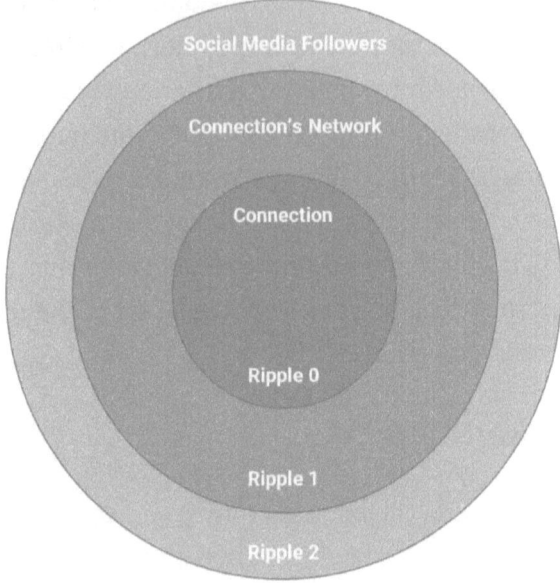

The personal brand may have a lot to deliver, but without the supportive network, it will be almost impossible to reach out to the broader audience. While the closest ripple wave is small, it consists of a few reliable connections. This group is familiar to you. Talking to them is like looking in the mirror. So apart from being a network multiplier, links are also best suited to give you feedback on personal branding aspirations. However, you need to think through the questions carefully. If you frame weak questions, they might be dismissed as frivolous.

They are also your best messengers. Not only are they capable of opening up access to their network, but they also promote you with lots of enthusiasm. Getting access to the network of your connections is the second ripple. This ripple will be much bigger than first. But it will still involve direct communication with people in the second ripple. You can approach them directly, just like your connections. Your first task with them will be to establish trust and credibility. It helps to keep some essential points ready when you talk to people in the second ripple.

Managing the ripple

For example, imagine 10 of your close connections giving access to 10 people from their network. With this, you will have access to 110 people to deal with in person. It will not be practical to manage so many connections along with your professional and personal life. This is when you start giving priority to those who will bring maximum benefit to you. But as the circle grows, even prioritization won't help after a while. And that's when you use social media to use its strengths.

Is it a sigh to finally encounter the word "*social media*" in the context of connections? We think most books create hype about how magically social media will enhance your branding.

Chemistry of networking

Peter Cook, a well-known author and coach, describes networking with the equation $S = N \times Q$, where S is your success as a networker, N is the number of connections, and Q as the quality of connections. Naturally, the quality of connections contributes majorly to access to a host of opportunities with jobs, promotions, investors, and customers.

The quality of connections can be viewed as chemical bonds.

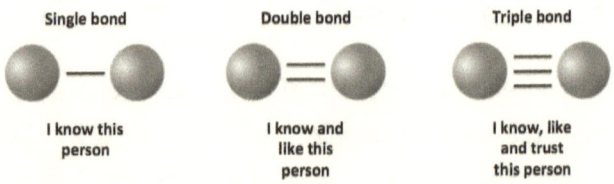

The higher level of bond means a lasting relationship with the connection. All networking relations start with a single bond.

There is no guaranteed formula to be a successful networker. But as long as you keep these four things in mind, your chances of having a triple bond goes up significantly.

1. ***Listen:*** A good listener is a good learner. The faster you learn about connection, the sooner you will establish a valuable relationship.

2. ***Be honest:*** Smart people can catch falsehood fast. Once exposed to lying, your personal brand will get tarnished forever. Your connection has to trust you to refer you to someone.

3. ***Collaborate:*** A willingness to collaborate and support connections is essential as it builds trust and helps establish a healthy relationship.

4. ***Keep showing up:*** Important connections may able to spend much time with you. But that does not mean they don't want to. It is a good idea to occasionally write, call, or meet them.

You must be conscious of your connections expectations and adjust your behavior accordingly if you want to create a win-win environment that will build a valuable network.

NETWORKING WINS	NETWORKING SINS
Build triple bonds for maximum trust.	Build large numbers of single bonds.
Create value for your network before seeking personal gratification.	Expect miracles from brief and shallow encounters.
Reciprocate wherever possible and appropriate.	Take, take, take.
Use the full range of networking methods (face to face, social media, etc.).	Just use social media or *face to face* for networking.
Gently engage people at face to face networking events.	"Ambush" people at face to face networking events.
Give relationships time to grow.	Never follow up with initial contacts to develop relationships.
Be focused about your face to face networking goals but also open to serendipity.	Try to be everybody's friend.

Source:https://www.linkedin.com/pulse/chemistry-networking-peter-cook/

Making most of social media

Over the last several years, there has been an explosion of growth in social media platforms such as Facebook, Twitter, LinkedIn, YouTube, Instagram, Tiktok, and many others. Social media platforms have become an essential means of communication and entertainment. One can easily say that the era of social media is just getting started and the adoption of social media will only become stronger over a period of time. The whole world has seen the impact of the expansion of social media on personal branding and networking, and the rising stats speak for themselves.

Different platforms attract diverse audiences and content. So, the right platform for you will depend upon your field and personality.

Building an active follower network and a brand for yourself requires offline and online efforts. Earlier, we talked about how to start with connections. But the sheer volume of interactions on social channels by people in search of information, recommendations, and entertainment presents your ideas in front of millions. There are tons of opportunities to add value with your experience – even to delight by entertaining and making that connection can help build a person's relationship with you as a brand. These relationships create the foundation for you to become a thought leader.

When you come up with new ideas or if you ever find yourself stranded, your followers will help remind the rest of the world who they're rooting for. Followership is not something that you can stumble upon or buy. Followership is mainly earned over a period of time through continuous and positive engagement with your online network base. It is gained through experiences that teach and delight and through delivery of the highest value to followers.

Loyal followership is the ultimate aim of using social media in this case and through them, your efforts to build a brand can truly scale. It shows that your brand is doing such a fantastic job that your followers talk about it from rooftops, sharing their opinions and experiences with their networks. That sharing is the best marketing a personal brand can ask for.

Identifying potential followers is a vital first step. You can use several social tools along with your observations to help picking out the type of followers – the people who are likely to advocate your brand. You will want to figure out what is most important to those potential followers. What are they looking for? Are they excited by first access to your knowledge? Figure out what type of followers your brand attracts and find ways to reward them for their advocacy. It is important to note that the community of followers grows organically and things won't happen overnight. While your knowledge encourages people to subscribe to your platform, helping you put the right foot forward, relationships take time.

We assume that you are proficient with social media to some degree. We won't get into smaller details here. Let's look at the most critical things you must keep in mind when using social media.

Being consistent

Many media experts will tell you that publicity *done once* is as good as *none*. Don't ever get enamored by one excellent blog or post. It's a mistake a lot of budding thought leaders make and then wonder why their followership is dipping.

Regular posts increase your reach because every time someone likes or comments on your posts, their followers will see your content.

Most of you will have a full-time business or career at hand, but that should not become an excuse for not being creative and consistent. There are a couple of tricks you must know.

Reusing content: You can reuse social media posts on multiple platforms with time intervals. It not only ensures freshness but allows you to address the audience in different time zones.

Creating once: The other technique is to create multiple posts whenever you are free and then post them over a period of time. It may mean stealing personal time or weekends for some of you. But this is a small price to pay for becoming someone your followers will love.

Staying relevant: Your views on the latest movie are unnecessary if you are vying to position as *Human Resources* guru. If the government has announced new changes in labor policy, then it will provide a perfect opportunity for you to write a post. It will increase your exposure as a lot of relevant audiences will be searching for the right information from the right source.

Talking about quality versus quantity of posts, it will depend upon your target audience's information consumption pattern. A public persona will be required to post several times a day, while if you post on serious topics, then a couple of posts a week are fine.

There is no hard and fast rule and you shouldn't subscribe to any of them either. As you progress, you will figure out the best pattern for your unique situation. Typically, smaller posts, comments, and likes should occur frequently. The long reads like a blog or article can happen at least once a month.

Social media analytics

Unfortunately, even regular users are not aware of the fact the social media sites provide basic analytics on post views for free. It can be quite useful information to access and know how many people follow you, from what segment, and what their expectations are. You can also see the content that has received high engagements and will, therefore, know to share similar types of content more often. On the other hand, content that has received timid response should also provoke introspection. Think about what is missing? Is it the message, tone, or timing? Then change these variables until an adequate number of engagements are received. Keep experimenting!

Overcoming objections

As your network grows, you will often meet naysayers in both the online and offline worlds. You will soon observe two peculiar trends. First, your content will be scrutinized closely for consistency of thoughts. And second, people will spare no opportunity to be critical of your opinion. Your first instinct may be to give a fitting response, but remember that any public spat may harm your brand. So be thoughtful of where and when you respond.

Here are four of the most common personalities who can be critical along with the potential response.

The Geeks: They will criticize objectively. The best approach is to work with them.

Likely to say: *"The year-on-year growth numbers are wrong. Please don't mislead readers."*

Proper response: *"Thanks for pointing it out. The numbers are from the Agriculture Journal, July 2018 issue. While I cross-check, why don't you share your source too?"*

The Quizzers: They will challenge you without any substantial proof. Acknowledge their emotions.

Likely to say: *"I don't agree that Renewable power is the only solution to our environmental problems."*

Proper response: *"I agree. There will be multiple ways to safeguard our planet's future. Please share what's on your mind so I and others can benefit."*

The Ranters: These people are highly opinionated, and no amount of explanation can calm them.

Likely to say: *"White cars are better than red."*

Proper response: *"While each individual will have their choice of color, White is among my favorite colors. Nice to see our choice matches."*

The Bully: Irrelevant responses, sometimes in offensive language.

Likely to say: *"I would have read the blog if you were not so ugly."*

Proper response: Ignore. Block or report the user if required.

The above samples are only to show how politically correct responses can be. The actual ones will depend upon your personality. The only precaution we urge you to take is – do not offend your followers!

Keep up the momentum

To what looks like madness, there's a method behind building connections and converting them into loyal followership. The process includes both offline and online activities. Some people give up midway because they expect significant changes overnight. You will have to be patient and disciplined to grow your connections steadily.

Remember that when your connections and social media posts grow, you will start receiving more attention. As a result, in the physical world, you will be invited for meets and in the virtual world, you will notice a higher number of interactions on your posts. One feeds into another. Pre and post-event posts on social media will reinforce your brand in the readers' or followers' minds. And not surprisingly, higher visibility in the physical world will impact the online following.

The habit of striving to expand the network in a disciplined manner will keep you ahead in the game and all you have to do is to keep up the momentum!

KEY TAKEAWAYS

- Having a large number of genuine followers, subscribers and friends on social media is one of the crucial factors in personal branding efforts.

- Loyal followers help you elevate your social or personal standing. They will stick with you in the face of competition.

- The journey usually begins in an offline mode before you attract an audience to your website or blog.

- Your network is like concentric waves around you. Potent messages produce significant and long-lasting waves.

- You can earn great followership over time through continuous and positive engagement.

- Use web analytics to understand audience engagement and develop your content strategy based on that.

- Do not expect significant changes overnight. Be patient and disciplined, grow your connections steadily.

8 | APPEARANCE MATTERS

The first 15 seconds are crucial when someone sees you for the very first time. They create your mental image in their brain, which they fine-tune over time, based on your interactions.

Most of us consider appearance only as the way we look. It is far more complicated than that. It is nonverbal communication that we do with the audience or, in other words, what is known as body language. A positive appearance can add immensely to your brand.

What is appearance?

Appearance is the image of you in the physical or virtual world as perceived by others. People notice your dressing style, observe your etiquette, and note your grooming. Ironically, most people will judge you within the first few seconds of their interaction with you. Those who are in fleeting situations such as a date or an interview may be at risk of being judged too quickly. But those on a long journey to build a personal brand will get little more breathing space.

A personal brand would want you to submit your best self to the world. The appearance that you present speaks to that. All of us have positive and negative sides. We keep striving to rectify the negative traits and try to project ourselves as a better and more presentable human being.

A colleague of one of the authors here was a chronic nose picker. The moment his brain got in a thinking mode, his fingers would subconsciously run toward the nose. It was a weird habit and would turn off a lot of prospects. But the nose picker was a brilliant technical analyst and his presence in meetings would increase chances of sales closure multifold. So, our author friend and the analyst made a pact. Whenever the author saw finger movements, he would lift the mobile phone, indicating to the analyst that he needs to stop.

If we keep the weirdness of the story aside for the moment, one cannot ignore the fact some habits are so deeply entrenched that no amount of practice can help get rid of them. These small imperfections make us what we are. Well, this book has repeatedly asked the readers to be genuine in their story and communication and the same applies to your appearance too. Our objective is not to critique you on your appearance, but just to handhold toward building a better image before an audience.

Dress up your brand

First, we won't ask you to dress up like a model. The expectation is to ensure you are comfortable, yet your clothes positively contribute to your personal brand. So, you must understand the basics of a well-dressed individual. It begins by being realistic and honest with yourself about what suits your body and what doesn't. It may require you to spend time in dressing rooms, but create that look, own it, and wear it, no matter what time of the day.

Keep the following points in the back of your mind when you choose your clothing:

1. The clothing must reflect your warmth and energy, make you approachable, and project you to be a competent person.

2. To have a steady image in people's minds, you will need several pairs of similarly styled clothing. So, plan your budget accordingly.

3. Just like clothes, accessories like shoes, jewelry, and tie matter too. They give the impression of a rounded or complete appearance. Accessorize just enough, anything overly done will look boorish.

4. Small visual deviations, like a hat, or brooch, will build higher personal brand recall.

It doesn't matter what your occupation or personality is, your "dress code" will supplement your brand. To be a package, you will also need to appear well-groomed.

Grooming for success

Grooming is like your clothing, a powerful form of the nonverbal style of communication. Grooming reflects your well-being in terms of bodily health.

Although these things would seem trivial, they matter a lot. The clean and odor-free body shows your ability to pay attention to detail, which is an expected quality from a public figure. Maintaining your teeth, breath, hair, hands, nails, and sleeping well will make you look your best and make you confident and comfortable in the presence of people.

There are specific grooming expectations, which vary based on the target audience. There are higher chances of your target audience misjudging you on the following issues.

1. ***Tattoos:*** They have emerged as the accepted form of body art. Still, some communities will find excessive exposure to tattooing offensive.

2. ***Piercings:*** Similar to tattoos, excessive display of piercings is considered a negative professional appearance.

3. ***Skin exposure:*** There is a worldwide debate as to what is ostentatious or inappropriate clothing. All we can say is some cultures look down upon skin exposure. If that audience forms a part of the world in your target group, then think twice before posting that beach photo.

4. ***Dirty clothing:*** It's not just your body, but dirty clothing also contributes to personal odor.

5. **Wealth showoff:** The excessive display of wealth will keep your audience from connecting with you.

The list above may have sounded like coming from your parents. Think of them as things we thought our parents were wrong but later realized they were not.

Bet on etiquette

Etiquette in public and professional lives are determined by a list of unwritten rules that individuals are expected to follow. We have all been hammered with the list of etiquettes at home and school. However, not a single day goes without us noticing gross violation of some simple protocols. As a thought leader, your conduct must be appropriate to command respect. The list of etiquettes is too long to be followed diligently. There are a few basic practices that will gain you respect among your followers.

1. **Respect all:** Avoid being prejudiced against people of different colors, creed, nationality, and wealth. Blind hatred against someone is contrary to the analytical thinking ability that a thought leader is known for.

2. **Focus on punctuality:** The fast-paced life can sometimes pose challenges in keeping time commitments. Situational awareness

and planning can help you avoid most delays. Even if you are late, but if you have genuinely made efforts to reach on time, you will be appreciated by your audiences.

3. ***Keep away phones:*** People are glued to their phones irrespective of their situations. The worst time to use the phone is when someone is chatting with you. It's a disrespectful act toward people who are trying to communicate because you wouldn't like someone to do it to you either.

4. ***Other important manners:*** Focus your attention during meetings, respond promptly to emails and social media posts – applauding people who support you are some essential gestures that will gain appreciation.

Social media appearances

Everything you post on social media has an infinite lifespan. No wonder, embarrassing posts keep resurfacing, even though they get deleted instantly by the writer. Thanks to the people with lightning screenshot skills and non-linear information flow on the Internet, a public figure cannot avoid being very careful when posting online content.

The following checklist of items should be a useful starting point:

1. ***Separate personal and professional network:*** The ideal way is to use different media platforms altogether. For example, some use Facebook for personal and LinkedIn for professional connections. If your target audience and personal connections are on the same platform, then create groups. All platforms let you create a private network or even closed groups.

2. ***Again, don't mix business and personal lives;*** it never works successfully.

3. ***Be cordial:*** Social media is the playground for posts that are against your personal/social/political beliefs. Typically, ignorance is the best policy since those posts are made just to evoke responses. But if you 'have' to respond, then graciously mention why you differ.

4. ***Acknowledge people:*** Actively follow your social media accounts to interact with your network. Respond quickly when someone asks a question, apologize if you offend someone, and do not ever spam, spread hatred, or trash someone else online.

5. ***Don't rush to post:*** Most of the embarrassing posts are made when someone rushes to make a judgment. Posting while drunk, sleepy, or depressed could lead to the same effect.

Always take your time to reflect on the content before posting.

6. ***Use correct grammar:*** Review your post for spelling and grammatical errors. Use free web plug-ins that are available freely online for spell check.

Get ready to go

Appearance is a small part of your overall personal branding strategy. Considering your aim to be a thought leader, adhering to the greater responsibility toward your dressing and etiquette shows attention to detail. Appearance, along with your values and personality, makes a complete package.

The list of considerations for a better appearance can be long. Don't get overwhelmed, apply commonsense rules, and get ready to go.

KEY TAKEAWAYS

- Being well-groomed indicates your seriousness about your objectives. Use your dress-code to supplement your brand.

- Grooming is a powerful form of the nonverbal style of communication. Grooming reflects your wellbeing and bodily health.

- Being meticulous at dressing and etiquette will show your attention to detail.

- Appearance, along with your values and personality, makes you a complete package.

- Your real-life appearances map your online activities. Be extremely careful when posting anything online.

9 | IMPORTANCE OF VISIBILITY

Nisha was a mediocre programmer. So, to pick up the slack, the manager asked Nisha to take up monthly reports, one of the most tedious tasks in the software outsourcing world.

Initially, Nisha was hesitant and even ashamed as she had seen the smirks on faces on a few of her colleagues when the announcement was made. But she had to take the reporting work if she had to remain in the team.

Month after month, Nisha lucidly reported pending items, open issues, and upcoming plans in the client call. And years later, when it came to downsizing the team, Nisha's manager without hesitation proposed her name. The client was surprised because he felt that the project would fail without her involvement. Soon, the client took some decisions and Nisha stayed on the team, replacing the current manager.

You may have experienced a similar situation at work or school and wondered how seemingly undeserving people get things going for them? The people who you think are undeserving may lack subject depth, but often have better communication skills than most others.

They understand the importance of *visibility* before the audience. In a professional setup, quite often, the audience is the decision-maker.

Visibility – what is it?

Let's do a small exercise. Think about your favorite topic and a person related to it. Now, try to describe the person in a few words. You will notice two different descriptors. One will be associated with this person's command over the topic and the other will be about that person's appearance. How often we hear things like "He is excellent at programming, but lacks dressing sense," or "She can use Excel like a pro, but only if she wasn't so arrogant."

Your visibility is the mix of your knowledge and appearance. Little expertise and a great character won't take you far. Similarly, people will stay away if you are knowledgeable, but have a wrong attitude.

Levels of visibility

We can categorize visibility in five progressive levels. Each level has a different focus, challenges, tools, and achievements.

- **Level 1** visible people are *Local Experts* who are known to close friends and colleagues. They aspire to build a personal brand outside the close circle and are ready to invest in self-development.

    They feel assured that their knowledge will be helpful to a broader audience and often regret that they did not invest in themselves and their careers sooner.

- **Level 2** people are *Community Stars* that are working on to increase their visibility, offline as well as online. Their reputation has moved beyond their circle and they are experiencing growing followership.

  These people are moving from generic expertise toward creating a niche. As they keenly follow audiences' feedback, they also observe specific patterns of better engagement. These experts have clearly understood the power of differentiation in the marketplace.

- **Level 3** people are often seen as *Content Commanders at a regional level*. They have built their unique style of thought leadership and they regularly invest in self-promotions.

  Most of them can be seen on top of their game with immaculate communication skills and crisp messaging. They use the Internet to the fullest for content distribution and self-promotion. These people also get regular speaking opportunities that are attended by a large number of audiences.

- **Level 4**s are typically *Big Bosses* who are the top authority in their areas of expertise. Each word they say matters to the industry. Senior decision-makers throw their doors open to meet such personalities.

They do not run after speaking engagements. They chose their venues and audience. These people are also highly conscious of their reputation. Promotion efforts are often lower to a level of keeping the lights on. The focus is on writing great speeches, articles, and books.

- **Level 5** people are *Veteran Thinkers* who have been there and done that. They have taken a back seat to make way for the new blood. However, masses associate their name with their areas of expertise.

  Veteran Thinkers can be on any prestigious visibility platform of their wish. They may not hold many groundbreaking thoughts in the field. However, the media frequently mentions them for their past work.

Most of you might find yourself at Level 1. A very few people get to taste fruits of Level 5. For career advancement and brand building, and also not to get overwhelmed with the effort it requires, to begin with we suggest you aim for Level 3. You can see how this compares with the *Influential Thought Leadership* framework from chapter 2.

Three essential pillars of visibility are the venues where your audience visits, content strategy, and communication skills. Let's analyze them in-depth one by one.

Where to find your audience

Where you want to be visible will depend upon your goal. If you seek votes, then you must be seen at public gatherings. If you wish to be recognized professionally, then speaking during trade events should be your game.

Whatever your goal is, showing up there more often is certainly a good idea. One of the ways a salesman befriends prospects is just by showing up again and again where his prospective customers are present. The familiarity of faces makes people comfortable to open up.

There are legendary and sometimes weird stories about how salespeople met the prospective buyer. One of our favorites is about Ravi, a salesman who would hang around the smoking zone at corporate events with extra cigarettes and lighters. Executives who were looking for someone to lend them cigarettes were Ravi's easy picks. They say that smoking induces *"feel good"* chemicals in the brain. Those five dedicated minutes with happy and grateful executives gave Ravi an excellent opportunity to meet, and exceed his goals consistently.

Now, we neither smoke nor encourage smoking. This story was included only to illustrate how some people can be creative in building their visibility by carefully studying habits of their prospects.

Forums that you choose could be offline or online. Both have their pros and cons. Online lets you reach a large number of audiences, while offline enables you to have a deeper connection. In other words, online is more efficient, while offline is more effective. You will find a mix of both to be very useful. It's like music artistes who release their work online but undertake promotional tours or a painter who promotes physical painting online.

Content matters

"Story, as it turns out, was crucial to our evolution – more so than opposable thumbs. Opposable thumbs let us hang on; the story told us what to hang on to."

– Lisa Cron

We want to reiterate that if you don't have stories, you can't impress the audience. All of the visibility in the world won't save you and people will quickly see through the bubble.

The content of the story should be continuously improving according to the feedback and changing tastes of the audience. Your resolve has to bring success to your audience by way of your stories.

Content strategy

As a thought leader, you can employ a variety of methods to reach your audience:

- Long-form writing - blog posts, articles, whitepapers, and books.

- Short-form writing - social media posts and reviews.

- Speaking engagements - including keynotes, webinars, podcasts, and interviews.

- Networking activities and relationship building.

- Search engine marketing.

The content strategy for personal branding doesn't have to be as comprehensive as that of a corporation's content marketing strategy. A small checklist will ensure that you are following the right path.

A sample checklist:

- What is my goal with the content strategy?

- Which type of content is the best to express my thoughts?

- What is the minimum number of artifacts needed periodically to make progress?

- What is my plan to produce the required artifacts?

- Should I consider taking external support to speed up my journey?

The above list is an indicative one, so go on adding checks that matter to you. It will be beneficial to have all your concerns answered and a plan in place before jumping into the production of content.

Sharpen your communication

With just your content strategy in place, you would next expect to communicate your story. You will want to influence your audience to view you like the brand you always wanted to be.

However, not everyone is a naturally gifted public writer, visualizer, or speaker. You must identify weaknesses and plan to take this challenge head-on. The good news is communication skills can be learned with practice or with some expert coaching.

Remember that multiple personal brands are trying to connect with your target audience. There's no doubt that your communication has to standout. Here are some tips to add sauce to your communication skills.

Be yourself

As easy as it may sound, you must have a unique communication style. It will make it easier for your audience to remember you.

Be creative

The other thing that will set you apart from others is your creativity. Better creativity will make your communication more engaging and attention-grabbing. For example, if your competitors heavily use only blogs, then you can differentiate your communication using visuals or voice.

Just remember one thing – creativity without value is useless!

Creativity without value is useless!

Be relatable

Keep the target audience on top of your mind when developing your content. Think of the problems they are trying to solve and how your communication can impact their lives. Your empathy will make your audience to like you more and share your content with their friends.

Let's revisit Nisha's story in the context of creativity. She made her reporting enjoyable by replacing tables with charts. She always gave importance to things which the customer had prioritized and delivered failures with potential workarounds. The customer enjoyed Nisha's youthful exuberance, clear communication, and entertaining commentary. It is not surprising that

Nisha not only stayed in the team during downsizing but also took up a more prominent role.

Take a plunge

The journey toward personal brand building is full of hard work and patience. It will involve learning new skills and committing several hours each week to perfect the trade.

The decision to invest your time and money in building visibility will certainly take willpower, but the choice is to live in obscurity or let the world know you.

Andy Mochan was a Superintendent on the Piper Alpha oil-drilling platform in the North Sea off the coast of Scotland. On a July evening in 1988, he woke up hearing loud explosions and alarms in his cabin. The outside was devastated with the oil platform burning in all its fury. Andy was severely injured, but he managed to run toward the edge of the platform. At that moment, he had two choices before him: to stay on the platform and hope for some miracle to save him, or to jump 15 stories in the water full of surfaced burning oil. Andy knew that he couldn't stay in the debris-laden freezing water for more than 20 minutes. Despite all that, Andy jumped from the platform to the sea.

He was soon picked up by a rescue crew, while others were not so lucky. The final death toll included 166 crew members and two rescuers.

Later, when they interviewed Andy from the hospital bed, he didn't mince words about his potentially fatal leap. *"It was either jump or fry,"* he said. Andy chose possible death over certain death. A lesson for us to remember when choices are tough – the price of staying on the "platform" is always too high.

When decisions are tough – the price of staying on the "platform" is always too high.

The way to the top isn't easy. However, if you decide to take a plunge, stay committed. If you are persistent, then small changes will undoubtedly be visible within days. Consider seeking professional help to speed up your progress if your situation permits. Having an expert on your side who can build your visibility strategy and help you navigate through challenging periods will benefit.

We hope this chapter has helped you to decode why certain people enjoy fame and popularity. We also hope to see you become one soon.

KEY TAKEAWAYS

- Better communication skills often precede subject matter depth.

- Visibility is an appropriate mix of knowledge and appearance.

- The venues your audience visits, the content they consume and your communication skills are the three crucial pillars of visibility.

- Without stories, it is difficult to capture the attention of your audience.

- Identify your communication weaknesses and take this challenge head-on. Communication skills can be learned with practice or with some expert coaching.

- Avoid living in obscurity and let the world know you. Invest your time and money in building visibility.

- It is a good idea to have an expert on your side to help you with visibility strategy and to help in navigating through challenging times.

10 | FROM TODAY ONWARDS

Several years ago, in May, Anand had an interview at LG for his dream job in R&D. A day before the meeting, the recruiting consultant called him and asked, "Are you nervous?" Anand said, "Of course, I am. But I do not doubt my capabilities." He continued, "I have been longing for this job for the last seven years, and I don't know if I would get it or not." The consultant reassured him that he had all the qualifications and experience that the job demands, so he would be okay. "So, I have this one last question," said Anand and asked, "If they ask me, why should we select you, what should I say," The consultant smiled and said, "Be confident, and tell them, if it's not you, then who?"

The last line did the job, and with tremendous confidence, Anand appeared for that interview the following day to win it. And sure, he did!

When he reflects on this story, he categorically remembers and asserts that the last sentence said by the consultant indeed made a profound impact. He still believes that it was perhaps the single most important thing that helped him in overcoming his imposter syndrome and limited beliefs.

After all, whether it is a self-upgrade, personal branding, or self-actualization, it all depends on your deep conviction. If you don't have it, you won't achieve it. It's that simple.

It all depends on your deep conviction. If you don't have one, you won't achieve it!

I've done all this, now what?

Now that you have read the book, we take it that you have thoroughly understood the foundations of personal upgrade and branding.

So, now we have an essential question to ask, *"What do you think that you can do next?"*

Well, it was a tricky question. You know what your answer to that transparent tricky question should be. Understanding foundational elements is just the beginning. Now there are two big tasks ahead of you.

The first one is to upgrade yourself and build and enhance your brand as well as reputation.

And the second, after you finish the first part, is to maintain the *"New You"* and live up to promises that your new version is making. Don't just do it for your career; do it for yourself, your entire life.

Throughout the book, we have tried to use and address *personal branding* in a prudent and calculated manner. We understand that it has become a buzzword with too many armchair experts, who claim to know all. There is a fine line between knowing something in theory and doing something in practice. A large part of today's world still believes that learning can happen from Google searches and Wikipedia reads. Unfortunately, that will only make you an armchair expert. Fundamentally, it doesn't equip the reader with wisdom. Wisdom is the quality that is needed to differentiate between right and wrong, good, and bad, as well as average, and the best.

There are many things that no one will tell you about personal branding and reputation management. Some people don't know about it and some don't want to give all the information (even if paid for). Whatever the reason, you must watch out for such pitfalls.

Things that no one tells

Several personal branding experts will tell you many of the steps you need to take to build your brand and how to maintain it.

But they will not tell you that your brand may also land in a lot of hot water, knowingly, or unknowingly. And if at all that happens, you must know how to prevent it from getting cooked up further. Many brand disasters are the product of distrust or doubt, and sometimes misinformation, and miscommunication.

Something might happen, which can make your target audience doubt your identity and make them wonder, "Who are you?" You might do something that would appear as hypocritical or inauthentic. You may not have done it intentionally, but that wouldn't matter. The problem with any negative news and gossip is, it spreads much faster than a good word of mouth publicity.

And mind you, the issue doesn't have to be something of a scandalous nature. It usually is relatively trivial, but questionable from your value system's perspective. It could be that you may have breached a contract inadvertently. Or maybe you said something in public that you signed up not to say or may have offended someone in a position of power? Perhaps your service didn't deliver promised results and none of that was your fault. Maybe it is the content that you posted online that appears to be plagiarized. Or someone signed up for your newsletter, then forgot about it, and told everyone that you spam them after they received one newsletter from you.

At the surface level, none of this could be significant enough to impact your reputation or branding in any way. However, what will affect it is how you respond to it. If you merely let it take its course, it may go out of control and do more damage than good. Responding quickly is the key element here.

You are not a celebrity or politician to cash-in on bad publicity. *"Any publicity is good publicity"* – this is terrible advice in your context. Plain denial can make things worse. Instead, first acknowledge the issue –

you don't have to accept it, only acknowledge it. Let everyone know that you are on it. Then investigate and clarify with the aggrieved party if there were any misunderstandings. If you think appropriate, then compensate them.

If it was your mistake, take full responsibility for it. Act to correct the mistake and apologize. We know that it is easier said than done. Regardless, one must do it no matter what, it is not an option.

Of course, we are not legal specialists or lawyers, so this may not work in some cases. Well, then you know your first point of contact should be your legal advisor. That, in our opinion, would only happen in extreme scenarios. But it is not impossible.

In the well-connected world, all it takes is 280 characters (of tweet) to put your brand at risk. So be careful. If you think that there might be anything online that could work against your new branding, work on it to get it removed or keep explanations handy.

We are not saying that you need to act and behave like a high-profile personality from day one. However, when it comes to personal reputation, your public-facing acts must always be cautious and thoughtful.

Almost no one tells you that when you build your brand, it goes public, always. And, so you have a responsibility to live up to its promises.

Thought leadership & personal brand

Throughout this book, we have emphasized on thought leadership as one of the methods to shine your brand. Many people, especially the ones from marketing fraternity, will tell you that personal branding and thought leadership are the same. However, from a purist perspective, they are very distinct aspects. We agree that they are two different things, but also think that there is significant overlap.

Ultimately, branding yourself is all about carefully crafting and creating a particular association or an image that people have about you when they hear your name or about you. Thought leadership, on the contrary, is about leading with ideas and thoughts that are valuable and useful in life. Thought leadership promotes new ways of thinking, new ways of looking at life or business or both.

So, yes – there is a connection between the two, and it can be a bit confusing due to mixed perspectives. This confusion usually comes from the fact that personal branding experts generally insist on carving out a niche and work in that specific area for content creation. In our experience, it is a somewhat lopsided approach.

With your brand, you can create content in two different ways to serve your followers or audience. One way is to curate useful and relevant information and to disseminate it appropriately. The second is by creating that information all by yourself, then distributing it directly, and through your support system.

Which approach is better, do you think?

When you use the information generated by others, you are merely a curator. It will rarely be your intellectual property. On the contrary, thought leadership is all about original thinking and the provision of new ideas. It comes from the thought leader's in-depth study and research in a particular area of expertise. Which means, thought leaders usually have the knowledge that others don't have.

"If I have seen further than others, it is by standing upon the shoulders of giants."

– Isaac Newton

If you are starting on the journey, you may curate content from others. It is a quick way to start your journey.

However, do not hang on to it for too long. Start creating your content, imbibe fresh thinking, and acquire new perspectives in your chosen field. Doing this will give you the best of both worlds. If you build thought leadership and personal brand together, you will be able to sustain longer, forever.

It's about time, not timing

Personal branding, especially if you choose to do it with thought leadership as a base, is not a short-term activity or project. There is no winning or losing. There is no end date to it.

If it is going to take nine months, it will take nine months. It doesn't matter when you start, it will still take nine months. Then, why wait and waste time? Get over with it and start now! The price you pay for not doing anything is too high. For doing nothing, you will pay with a daily dose of frustration, constant feeling that something is missing out in your life, without realizing what it is and, more importantly, limiting yourself from your true potential. Can you imagine the feeling that you might get after many years, and you will think, "What if I could have at least tried?"

It is not about timing, it is about time you put in to build it.

When you are building your reputation, it is for your lifetime. Take all the time needed to build it right and permanent. Play the infinite game!

Consistency is one of the critical aspects and it can't be achieved with short blips, it has to be done over a longer period. It is not about timing, it is about time you put in to build it.

You'll know when you're succeeding

One of the frustrating issues, primarily when you work on the long-term, is getting the feedback. Knowing when things are working for you and when they are not.

Your brand is an implied promise to your audience, to everyone around you. When you live up to it, you will see relationships getting better and healthier. That is one of the primary indicators. People at work and off work will start to see more of the real you. In our experience, people appreciate a more cut and dry personality if it is genuine, as against phonies or sycophants. In short, authenticity wins. And you will start to see that incremental change in a few weeks as you start working on it.

More importantly, you will be satisfied and peaceful with whatever you are doing as a result of it. Instead of getting frustrated with trying to continually adapt to some of the unreasonable demands of your external world, you will be content with what you are doing because everything will come from your core. You will feel centered and grounded.

At the same time, you will also feel quietly confident, which will emanate from your hard work in putting together your brand.

Tangible results may take time to be visible as they are mainly the function of several unknown and uncontrollable factors of life. Nonetheless, things will be better than before.

Where to find more resources?

We have worked extensively to make sure that we provide enough information and inputs to help you start working on your brand. Nonetheless, this by itself is not an all-in-all guide. You will need many resources as you progress to refer to and use in your endeavors.

Given that there is a lot of junk out on the Internet (and offline too), you will have to be extremely cautious. You need to be picky about what you refer to and who do you listen to. A lot of people come from their vested interests, which may be useful for them but difficult for you. Many people would use your ignorance to sell you something, usually things that you would never need or don't need now.

In all that noisy world, we think books are the best and should be your first point of reference. A well-researched book from reputed authors is worth more than its price. You should shortlist books based on your area of interest and thought leadership as well as the brand element that you are trying to improve.

After books, we highly rank personal coaching and mentoring from people who have built their brand all by themselves and are thought leaders in their chosen field. They may or may not be professional coaches or mentors and that shouldn't matter. Having built a personal brand without piggybacking on someone else's brand is an excellent testimony. These people may coach you or mentor you on a one-on-one basis. Some of them might also be doing that with a group of people through their Master Classes. Either way, we think it can be a good investment, as long as you do your due diligence.

Most importantly, pay for all the resources you get and all the support you seek. It goes against the grain of conventional thinking that everything is free on the Internet. If everything is free, you must ask, *"What is the value that it adds?"* and *"In what other ways am I paying for it?"* For example, if you go with DIY type of information, it is typically available for free, but you need to put a lot of time, resources, and efforts to do everything yourself. Essentially, you are paying for that free information with your time and resources. So, think carefully about what type of value exchange is happening and if that is acceptable to you.

Be wary of social media hacks, you may need them sometimes, but that's not your priority. Outcomes achieved from hacks usually do not last long. Remember you are supposed to play an infinite game, you have all your life ahead of you to work on it. You don't need short cuts.

If you are searching for information online, usually, you should find multiple resources and points of view on each topic. Then cross-reference them and see where they match or don't match. Doing that itself reveals exciting trends, and you will be able to discern the fluff from value.

From today onwards

Don't just upgrade yourself and build a personal brand, live it!

It is the most important and easiest thing that you can do, starting today. Once you have discovered your inner values and strengths, maximize on them. Cautiously reflect your authentic self at all times and see the difference. When your personality and brand is reflecting your true passions, lifestyle, and persona, you will exhibit quiet confidence, which is just right, and vital.

You will soon discover that when you start your personality upgrade from authentic roots, it is not only comfortable but also fun and a self-fulfilling experience. As a result, you will do a better job of making it happen.

If you want to exhibit a personal brand for being an intellectual, you must show that through your actions. Take part in all intellectual challenges and showcase them. If your brand has an artistic angle, show that through your creative prowess. If it is about people, be outgoing.

In short, be your brand. Live it, every single day. At home, at work, at events, in public places... everywhere!

Have a deep conviction that you have a tremendous value to offer. But first, you must decide to act on it. And, then, you need to do it.

It is time to invest time, energy, and money into doing the highest value activities for you. It won't be easy, but it will be worth it.

Upgrading yourself is a big decision, and yet it is a choice that you have to make soon.

So, make it!

Because, if it's not you, then who?

If it's not you, then who?

KEY TAKEAWAYS

- What you do from today onwards for upgrading yourself depends on your deep conviction. If you don't have it, you won't achieve it.

- Wisdom is the quality that is needed to differentiate between right from wrong, good or bad and average from the best. You can't get that from just Google and Wikipedia, you have to work for it.

- Always keep your public-facing acts cautious and thoughtful.

- If you build thought-leadership and personal brand together, you will be able to sustain longer, maybe forever.

- When it comes to personal branding or thought-leadership, it is not about timing, it is about the time you put in to build it.

- Many people use your ignorance to sell you something – usually, things that you don't need now or the ones you would never need.

- Play an infinite game, there is no deadline, and you don't need short-cuts.

- When your personality and brand reflects your true passions, lifestyle, and persona, you will exhibit quiet confidence, which is just right and vital.

- Don't just upgrade yourself and build a personal brand, live it! And always remember – *if it's not you, then who?*

ABOUT THE AUTHORS

Anand Tamboli

Anand is a serial entrepreneur, global speaker, award-winning author, innovator, and transformation specialist.

For people seeking accelerated personal transformation, Anand provides clear and practical strategies that successfully work in real life. He is a polymath who brings unique perspectives on topics that people think are "done to death."

When working with several Fortune 500 multinationals, Anand gained extensive cross-industry and multi-cultural experience. He specializes in areas that intersect with technology and people.

As an intense spiritual seeker, Anand loves to talk about core systems that shape our lives, such as education, work, politics, parenting, and spirituality.

Know more about him at *https://www.anandtamboli.com/story.*

Amit Danglé

Amit is just like the city where he was born, Mumbai. He is imperfect, open-minded, hardworking, but most importantly, resilient. The death of his first son or the financial lows created by his decision to do full-time social work didn't keep him down for long.

The greatest and, perhaps, the only skill Amit holds is storytelling. Give him the most ordinary situation and he will create Macbeth. Naturally, Amit can find himself professionally contributing as a marketer. For about two decades, he has helped several multinational companies build brands their audiences can trust.

Amit's latest endeavor is to promote personal branding among fellow professionals so they can achieve their life goals. He likes to mix his corporate branding experience with human values to create a tantalizing approach that everyone can follow.

Know more about him at *https://www.linkedin. com/in/amitdangle/*.